I'M NOT OK.
YOU'RE NOT OK.
BUT IT'S OK!

Chris Padgett

 DynamicCatholic.com
Be Bold. Be Catholic.®

I'M NOT OK. YOU'RE NOT OK.
BUT IT'S OK!

Printed in the United States of America.[1]

ISBN: 978-1-937509-77-4

Dynamic Catholic® and Be Bold. Be Catholic.®
and The Best Version of Yourself® are registered trademarks
of The Dynamic Catholic Institute.

Design by Jenny Miller

For more information on this title
and other books and CDs available through
the Dynamic Catholic Book Program, please visit:
www.DynamicCatholic.com

The Dynamic Catholic Institute
5081 Olympic Blvd
Erlanger, Kentucky 41018
Phone 1–859–980–7900
Email: info@DynamicCatholic.com

TABLE OF CONTENTS

Introduction 7

1 The Difficulty of Relationships 15

2 Is There a Meaning to Our lives? 47

3 The Wound 59

4 Self-preservation 71

5 The Weight 85

6 The Want.. 99

7 Be Needy: Recognizing Our Need
   Is the Beginning of Healing 113

8 Risk it: Be Vulnerable 123

9 Christ In Us 133

10 The Cross 143

Conclusion... 155

SPECIAL THANKS TO:

Linda Padgett
Hannah, Sarah, Madeline, Mary, Ella
Noah, Kolbe, Jude, and Joseph

I am grateful for Matthew Kelly's adventurous spirit
in collaborating with me in ministry.

To all of my friends and ministry partners,
thank you for loving me even though I am so disturbed.

A WORD OF ADVICE:

At the end of each chapter are questions for potential personal or group reflection. Some of them may be too personal for you to disclose, so feel free to modify them as you wish. These are only meant to encourage you to think deeper about the material and to prompt discussion. There is also a recommended reading portion, and I would encourage you to suggest other great books that have helped you along the way. Happy reading, my friends.

INTRODUCTION

I'M NOT OK

Anyone who knows me probably won't find that statement surprising. My wife regularly reminds me that I often have the mind of a fourteen-year-old boy. What she doesn't realize is that most men have the same mentality. Women everywhere, I imagine, are nodding their heads in agreement. Beyond the basic propensity for juvenile behavior, I think the older I get the more I realize that I am not getting the hang of this thing called life. While I realize I am light years beyond some of the struggles I dealt with as a teen, I also find that I am now just as distracted and prone to failing as an adult. Over the years, struggles I was certain I had tackled in terms of personal flaws and vices have reared their ugly head, haunting me once again. I am not OK. Often I find that while I know more now about life and the faith than I ever did as a kid, I seem to struggle to live this faith more now that I am an adult. I want to do great acts of charity, speak calmly to my children, and live with heroic virtue, but so often I fall short. I desire to be a holy man, but I seem to be excelling at being average instead of in spiritual maturity. I am an expert in self-loathing, I struggle with feeling insecure and depressed, and while I am sure a lot of it is explained by my childhood, I've often wished I could just move on and be the great man I know God wants me to be. I keep hearing about God as loving and tolerant, but I often feel I am without excuse, and I can honestly say that there are days when I am tempted to despair of ever being what I need to be as a man, father, husband, son, and child of God. So I think it is important to let you know that I do not feel like I have all the answers to life's problems, nor am I sitting back amazed at the difficulties people have in living the faith. I am right there with you, wanting to know more about a God who sees that I am not OK and wants to be with me anyway. Wouldn't that be a great truth?

YOU'RE NOT OK

While I don't know you personally, I am 100 percent confident that you are not OK. Life is so difficult, with familial obligations, neighborhood drama, work responsibilities, and personal struggles all seeming to overwhelm us without relief or restraint. We might want to pretend that all is well, but I have a feeling if you were to stop and just ask yourself how you are doing, the vast majority of you would say that you are hanging on by a thread. You are not OK, and yet you continue to press forward, concluding like everyone else that this is probably as good as it gets.

I remember hearing about a very well-known theologian who got a divorce, and the feeling many of us had was one of utter shock. In many ways I thought his marriage and family life was one that was worthy of imitation, only to find out that he and his wife were not OK. In fact, so many friends of mine who have been brought up in the Church have either gotten divorced or have remained in marriages in which they often feel unloved, unheard, and unable to move beyond basic tolerance of one another.

You are not OK, and the braver you are in facing this truth, the faster you can find and embrace a solution. Whether it is financial chaos brought on by unforeseen events or poor money management, or familial bickering, many of you feel that it is almost pointless to try anymore, since nothing ever changes. There is a desperation to your day as you wonder if you will get the job you've applied for, the raise in salary that you deserve, the attention from a spouse who seems to find interest in everyone but you, and when these moments end in loss, it often seems we knew failure was awaiting us at every turn. You are not OK as you hear people speak poorly about your family and make remarks that hurt you personally, and as you struggle internally with insecurities and depression, knowing that you are not what you want to be. You are not OK in more ways than you could have imagined, but I want you to know that it's OK.

BUT IT'S OK

What if life could be lived differently? What if an awareness of why we struggle, along with a hope of how to achieve victory, could actually be attained? What if it were OK for us not to be OK, not to be perfect and have it all together? What if we could honestly just be who God made us to be, flaws and all, and simply take a break from all our games and protective habits?

One day a number of years ago, I stumbled into an adoration chapel, extremely frustrated with my walk with God. I'd been struggling with a lot of personal vices, finding little to no victory in my spiritual life, and I was slated to give a talk to thousands of youth. I felt like I had nothing to give. The keynotes I had given in previous years had been remarkable; they seemed to have gotten better and better over the past few years. But as I knelt in the tiny chapel before Jesus, I felt like I had nothing of value to give. What if I failed? What if I couldn't connect effectively with the teens and the adults who'd brought them to the event? What if I didn't get hired to come back the following year? I was extremely frustrated with myself, and unable to come up with a new and catchy idea to wow the crowd. I was just a mess. I remember telling Jesus that I had nothing to give, and really, what right did I have pretending otherwise? During those brief moments of vulnerable honesty I felt like Jesus reminded me that while I was yet a sinner, he had died for me. How much more did he love me now that I was longing for him and striving to live a life in honor of his call? In the end, I began to hold on to the idea that even if I failed, Jesus' love for me was what I needed. I was not OK. The reality, though, was that Christ was OK with me not being OK. I didn't have to wait for one day in the future when I would hopefully have my act together, because Jesus was truly with me in my imperfections.

Fast-forward a few years and I was sitting in a hotel room with a number of men who make their living doing music ministry and traveling the world giving keynotes at churches. In the room, we opened up about how broken we all felt at times.

We talked about how often we were tempted, how insecure we felt at certain events, how easy it was to compare ourselves even with each other. One gentleman shared about his struggle with pornography, and another shared about his struggles with drugs and alcohol. These were some very big figures in ministry, and I realized they also were not OK, but in Christ it was OK for all of us. It gave me a sense of relief to realize I was not alone, that ministers in the top tier were flawed like I was.

Recently I returned from a trip to the Netherlands, where I gave everything I had. I spoke to the adults and teens numerous times over the week I spent there, and while it was an amazing opportunity, I was drained. I had been on an insane summer schedule, living out of hotels more than it seemed I'd been living in my own home, accompanied by my travel companion, a battered suitcase with a zipper that may or may not work, depending on the day.

Immediately after that international event I flew to Arkansas and had a few talks to give before heading home for a long-awaited vacation. My wife had been with me in the Netherlands, but I missed my kids and missed my chair, my TV, my basement with all its books, and my dog, who had likely dropped a fragrant gift next to my desk to declare his irritation with my travels. I was simply worn out. I remember texting my wife and giving her updates like, "Only three more talks left." The Arkansas event ended with a prayer service, and I vividly recall sitting in the back of the room staring at all these older people who were raising their hands, soaking in the joy of the Lord. I was really apprehensive about the evening prayer service, because I realized that I didn't have what all these old-time charismatic Catholics were looking for. I wasn't a prophetic voice, a person who could read souls, or someone who got words of knowledge. I was a married man with lots of kids who needed to be in my home recovering from extensive travels. I remember telling Jesus—again—that I had absolutely nothing left to give. There was not one iota of emotion that I could hold on to in order to work myself up into some holy prayer. I didn't have any strong feelings about what I should emphasize in the evening service. I was the wrong guy for the job. What did I have to offer these veterans of the faith? That night I walked hesitantly to the front, and in a bit of a self-conscious daze I began to pray, and I kid you not, the Lord spoke through me. I was amazed, and those beautiful people were blessed. I was not OK, but it was OK because God always has a plan.

He has a plan for you, just as he has a plan for me, and while there are a million reasons why we can't be whole, can't do ministry, can't make a difference in our families, or simply can't function, there is but one truly good reason that we can and will: God has a plan. This book is a brief look at the plan he has for you and me, even though we have so many rough edges in our lives to smooth out. There will be a lot of insights that I can honestly say I am trying to apply in my own life. I am not giving you information because I know everything that needs to be done to live a great and holy life; rather, I am giving you the things that I myself am holding on to for dear life. And when I slip and fall, which I often do, I find that Jesus is holding on to me because he considers my life dear. What is this plan? If you will let me, I'd like to start by looking at the importance of relationships, and how they have aided in our struggle to be

OK—but don't be afraid, because God is bigger than our family chaos, bigger than our sin, and bigger than our circumstances. God's plan is exactly what you need to see and believe so that you can know everything really is going to be OK.

CHAPTER 1:
THE DIFFICULTY
OF RELATIONSHIPS

Everything we do involves a relationship of one type or another. From the family dynamic in which we have grown up to our friendships to the interactions with others even in the workplace, all require that we "play nice" with others. There are some relationships that we can pick on our own, but many of them we have no control over whatsoever. We can't choose our fellow employees, and it is likely that many of us have left jobs because of the intolerable working conditions. We can't control who our family members will be, even if we wish we could! There are times when factors beyond our control impact our basic relational structures, causing them to implode. Maybe we don't know our parents because of death or divorce, but you did have parents at one point in time, and they did impact your life in one way or another. Basic genetic makeup isn't something without incident, so while many don't know their parents, their lives were touched by them nonetheless. Attaining and maintaining healthy relationships is difficult. In this chapter I will look at three primary relationships and show how they either point us toward and aid us in our understanding of God, or detract from and hinder that most important relationship.

God has been trying to get our attention. He uses three basic relational pillars, or primordial structures, to assist us in knowing him. The first is parental, the second deals with friendship, and the third involves interactions and encounters with what I would term, our significant others. These pillars are meant to show us what love looks like. Love is not exclusive; rather, it is inclusive. While the world insists upon limitations on how love can function, Christian love should be limitless in terms of our willingness to accept and embrace one another regardless of our flaws. The world continues to wait with bated breath for the witness of love. In fact, the appeal and longing for love is so great that the hope of experiencing it often leads to conversion when an individual truly encounters it in followers of Christ. Even amid great obstacles in relationships with family, friends, and others, Christ is able to reach into the hungry heart and enable us to see and experience true love. The ideal is for us to have a framework of existing love that points us toward God. When this happens, the journey to knowing and loving God becomes so much easier.

Think of a small child playing with a basketball. At first the ball is too large and the young person's ability to control a pass or dribble the ball is limited. With time and practice, basic ball-handling skills are developed, but the child is by no means ready to play the game. Watching the sport on television is another way to let the principles of the game sink into the young athlete, but in the end, it is taking all that he has been given, the skills he has initially developed, and actually jumping into the game that allows for him to begin to become the player that he would like to be. When we look at these three primordial structures of love, they are meant to teach us how to hold the ball, how to dribble, and the mechanics, so that when we get to the point of playing the game we will be able to reach back into our arsenal of experience and apply it to the relationship in which we are made to excel.

1. FAMILY: MOTHER AND FATHER

When I was a young boy my family regularly traveled to Birmingham, Michigan, to celebrate Christmas with my grandparents. Most of us have fond memories of our grandparents, and usually one set, either the maternal or paternal, is a bit more accommodating to the grandchildren than the other. This holiday was celebrated with my paternal grandparents, and they knew just how to make their grandchildren feel special. When my sister and I would go grocery shopping with my grandmother, she would let me pick whatever sugary cereal I wanted. That was a big deal! Count Chocula, Franken Berry, Boo Berry, Frosted Flakes, and Cookie Crisp, a few of my favorites, were not only filled with an inexplicable amount of glorious sugar, but their commercials all displayed kids filled with great euphoria as they consumed bowl after bowl of their morning nourishment. Juxtapose this set of grandparents with my maternal grandmother and you can see why I favored the former over the latter.

Grandma Arda, my mother's mother, must have made an agreement with my mother and the area dentists to return home from the Red Owl grocery store with only healthy cereal, bringing my childhood trauma to unprecedented heights. Arda and my mother would bring home depressing boxes of Grape-Nuts, which for a small child was like eating a bowl of rocks, and if you let the milk settle in its nutty nastiness for a small period of time you could actually turn your breakfast bowl over and nothing would come out! No wonder we all struggled with irregularity! I think you can actually drywall with Grape-Nuts after it reaches that puttylike consistency. She also brought home Bran Flakes, which to me looked like a bowl of scabs. Do you remember puffed cereal? I think we used those puffs to pack up our dishes when we moved from North Dakota to our new home in South Dakota—after all, they had the same consistency as packing peanuts. I remember Shredded Wheat as well, and while many assume it had sugar on one side, back in the early '70s it came in what looked like a giant white feed bag containing a pallet-like slab of pressed wheat full of morning nutrition—which would have given a horse its daily allotment of hay. The prize was probably a package of Kleenex for all the children wailing in sorrow after having to eat it. Not appealing—in fact, in those lonely days we had to use our spoon to mash up the bale of cereal so that the shards of wheat wouldn't cut our throats as we consumed it. The worst cereal of all was simple bran cereal, which looked the same way going in as it did going out. There should have been a picture on the box of two senior citizens looking a bit panicky at one another with the caption, "The prize comes later!"

So you can imagine the joy I felt when I went to my paternal grandparents' house, where healthy cereal wasn't even on their radar. The prizes in sugary cereal boxes were for the most part incredibly useless, except for a record on the back of the Cookie Crisp box that you could cut out and actually play—but we didn't care! (For the younger audience, a record is a large vinyl disc that has music on it.) Not only could I eat whatever sugary cereals I found fitting for my experienced palate, but I was also allowed to drink Faygo, a drink sold in Michigan (I think it's outlawed in forty other states) that's basically the equivalent of crack for small children. The sugar content in that drink alone brings joy to dentists in the surrounding area and panic to any teen who has to babysit those sugar-crazed kids. I have wondered, if children drank enough of this carbonated happiness, would their urine actually glow in the dark? I'm afraid to drink it now, because I'd likely need to call my cardiologist and have him on standby in case the experiment went awry.

One day, a month away from my fifth birthday, during our vacation, while I was jacked up on mass quantities of sugar and caffeine, my father told me he wanted to speak with me. We made our way into the living room of my grandparents' house, and I would venture to guess the temperature in their home was a balmy 99 degrees. The heat in most elderly people's homes would cause any rock candy in the candy jar to fuse together, thereby making it impossible to select just one piece. My dad knelt down, looked me in the eye, and told me that after this Christmas vacation he wouldn't be living with us anymore. I didn't have a clue as to what he was talking about; in fact, I had better things to do, like play with the walkie-talkies we'd all gotten that Christmas.

When my mother, sister, and I arrived back at our home in North Dakota, I walked up to the screened back door, looking at the snow illuminated by the outside light in the frigid Dakota winter evening. Suddenly the door opened and my father looked out at us. I stared into his eyes and said with great childhood tact, "I thought you told me you weren't going to be here when I got home." We walked into the house that evening, and life continued seemingly as if nothing had taken place in Michigan. I don't know when he left, but I would guess it was only a matter of months. It probably happened one afternoon when I was at school, or during the night, when I was tucked in bed listening to the gerbils run endlessly on their spinning wheel. My father moved to the other end of town, into his own home, with his own plans and his new wife. This time there was no special word informing me of his departure. As I have reflected upon that day over the span of several decades, I've realized my understanding of what relationships can look like, especially parental love and unity, was forever changed. It would take me many years to try and put together a picture of what a faithful husband and regular fatherly presence within the home should look like.

My sister and I would visit my father on the weekends, but it was difficult for me to savor this special time with him, because another woman was there wanting his attention. In many ways I struggled with understanding the role my father's new wife, Gail, played in my life. One afternoon I wrote her a note with such simplicity I am sure Ernest Hemingway would have been proud. That literary masterpiece read, "I hate you." I saw her countenance fall as she read the note, and as a result I was filled with inexplicable guilt. I just wanted her to know that she didn't belong to me even if she now belonged to my father, and that I was not making room for her in my life. I hadn't intended to hurt her so much as make my feelings known. I decided to try and fix what I had done after I saw her pained face, and so I wrote a second note that read, "I love you." Of course, I didn't mean it, but I wanted to take back the hurt I had inflicted. She read the note and said to me, "Chris, I realize you are trying to make up for the previous note, but I want this to come from your heart and not because of your guilt. I want you to mean it if you say those words to me." In many ways I realized that I couldn't write that type of an affectionate note, at least in the way she desired, because I wanted my father to be back with my mother. I didn't want to share him with another woman, and I wasn't sure how to fix what I felt was broken in my parents' relationship. I am confident those were very difficult times for my stepmother, and we have had wonderful conversations as adults about those early years. She became a friend, and we both recognized that who we were within those family relational dynamics back then is not who we are today, and yet, those earlier moments have shaped our lives in varying degrees.

Having talked with Gail many years later, I realize we both would have done things much differently if we could have seen the consequences of our actions. These familial dysfunctions, specifically divorce, were not as common in those days, and its effect on one's perspective on God and the future was probably not written about with as much clarity back then as it is today. When I was in elementary school, I could find maybe one other student who came from a broken home. I felt alone and unable to articulate how frustrating it was not to be an agent of healing for my mother and father. I wanted to help them reconcile, but I was unfit for the task.

Years later I returned to North Dakota to give a talk and minister to the youth in that diocese. It was good to be back in the area I had grown up in, and as usual, the northern United States was one neurotic moment away from a blizzard. I was staying at a small hotel, probably one of the nicer ones in the area, but not as luxurious as most I'd been in throughout my global travels. Who really needs hot water? I spoke with a Native American gentleman in the lobby, who told me that when he was a small boy he watched his uncle accidentally shoot and kill his father with a gun they had been playing with. The event was still vivid in his memory, and it was told in a way that has caused it to be vivid in mine. While he functioned as an adult, that moment had forever impacted how he lived his life. He had been shaped by a moment in time that he had no control over. If he could have changed the past, he would have, but he was unable to bring his father back to life.

One of my professors at Palm Beach Atlantic College in southeast Florida had a wife who was going blind. Their life was never going to be the same, and while it seemed as if they were able to work past this hurdle together, I have often wondered how it would be to watch someone you care about slowly lose her ability to see. Sunsets, her children's faces, the wrinkles setting in over the years would all be memories instead of moments currently shared through the sense of sight. I know most of us are unable to fathom and relate to some of these events, but many people have carried the weight of disabilities and loss with little interest in wearing their past upon their sleeves for all to see.

A young college girl came to talk with me about her parents, and while nothing tragic had happened, she wished that they were more loving toward one another and their children. She was longing for a father who would pray with her and cheer her on, but too often she felt that she was meant to move forward in life toward adulthood without their concerned involvement. As we spoke I asked her about her grandparents, and the stories she told were about very difficult relationships that had unraveled over time. I looked at this young woman and said to her that it was likely that her parents felt their marriage was far better than anything they had experienced as children, so while she longed for more involvement from her mom and dad in her life, what she received from them was much more rich and beautiful than either parent would have imagined possible.

Every family has a story, and some are filled with trage- dy and pain, while others illustrate lives that seem to have been boring and without adventure. Each family brings a lot of baggage into the relational pillars, which adds to those hur- dles of difficulty and struggle. These stories show a variety of problems that unfortunately many can relate to within the family dynamic. Our parents, who often seem so constant and steady to our young minds, many times turn out to be indi- viduals who are far more vulnerable than we would have ever imagined. Children and parents react to these sobering mo- ments of difficulty in a number of ways: by building up walls to protect us from further hurt, by wearing masks so that we can pretend that nothing bothers us, or by numbing ourselves to the pain of our past. Fear manifests in a way that can be so paralyzing we seem to resort to primal protective avenues in order to survive. We will talk about this more in a later chapter, but what we will need to do is find a way to deal with the dysfunction we have experienced, whether severe or minor, in order to enable true healing in our lives. We can't change the past, but we can choose how to address these hurts, and identify the lies and obstacles to our healing process so that we can begin to move toward a better perspective. Without that healing we will often find ourselves unable to cope with the roles and responsibilities we now have as adults. While we may be unfit for the task of moving forward from such pain, in Christ we become fit for the task. We can be OK in Christ, even if our life experiences have made things overwhelmingly not OK.

For all of us, the parental impact can be positive or negative, and while many times our family dysfunction isn't that extreme, seeing it with a fresh perspective can allow us to intentionally choose different paths for our future. Maybe we had a mother who was obsessive-compulsive about cleaning. My mother seemed to do spring cleaning every week, as far as I could tell. We would regularly rearrange the furniture, which apparently made all the old furniture seem exciting until we would unexpectedly crash into corners of tables and chairs that were not there previously as we stumbled toward the bathroom with rapidly revealing bruises. She had us take the screens off the windows and spray them down regularly and vacuum our rugs more than I ever thought possible. Even more horrific than the constant cleaning of our home, we would have to bathe every day! Come on, Mom! These are not necessarily overt life-altering dysfunctions (except maybe the bathing part), but seeing these familial moments from a healthy perspective can help us to understand our current actions, obsessions, and apprehensions. I wonder if my mother's desire to constantly clean our small home in the Dakotas was a declaration, conscious or not, that at least with her children and that house she had an element of control over how we acted and how it looked. She certainly couldn't control the actions of her previous husband and the unraveling of her marriage, but those floors would be clean.

While our parents often struggle with their own issues and difficulties, if they can find a way to love each other in the trying moments, then they will leave their children with a foundation for their future. If our parents did their job right, by being a gift to one another and reflecting self-donation instead of selfishness, then they are in fact offering their family a glimpse into the love of the Trinity. If they were not able to find a way to remedy their own wounded selves, then the impact upon their children will be more difficult to move beyond. It is a little like that sporting analogy I previously mentioned. Many of our parents never learned how to dribble or pass the ball to achieve the success they wanted, and as a result the game came to a screeching halt.

Saint John Paul II says in *Familiaris Consortio* that marriage does three things: (1) it shows God's unshakable love for the world (till death do us part); (2) it shows Christ's love for the Church (lay down your lives for each other: husbands love your wives as Christ loves the Church); and (3) it will in fact change society, if it is holy. These points should instill in us as adults an awareness of the depth and impact marriage can have, but too often couples are more in survival mode, rather than thriving together.

Most of us come from homes that are probably a mix of good and bad moments. We have likely been surprised at ourselves when suddenly we realize that we have just acted like or said something our parents used to say. The idea of becoming our mothers or fathers can be haunting, especially if the past we experienced had many wounds from which we are still unable to adequately recover. In many cases individuals spend their entire lives trying to do things differently but without an understanding of what tools are needed for success. Often they have no concept of what a successful and thriving marriage can even look like, and so regularly couples end up embracing the pursuit of things and status, assuming that will be the answer to marital difficulties. If our parents did not love one another as couples could, or did not love their children properly, the result, unfortunately, was that many children were approaching adulthood without the skills needed for success.

In addition, the idea of God becomes muddied, with numerous insecurities, misunderstandings, and difficulties in relating to one who supposedly loves us as his children, or even sees members of the Church as his bride. Remember what Saint John Paul II says about a holy marriage: It will show the world God's unconditional love, because a husband and wife are willing to weather any storm and come out unified instead of divided. If that unified front is created and the foundation between them strengthens, their children will be given a gift of stability in viewing this primordial relationship, and the world will find that at least one relational institution is capable of enduring difficulties without completely imploding. It is possible that many families don't realize their gathering together is beyond two people living together, but is more a witness of what the heavenly community is like. We need to be reminded of the hope that we can strive for, and of the consolation and aid available to those battered by the casualties of broken marriages. I am spending a lot of time with this first pillar of relationships, because regardless of our vocation, we all have memories of a family dynamic that has either helped us to see God more clearly or hindered this perspective.

When a husband rejects his wife, it's almost impossible for the unwanted spouse to just move forward. Recently I was in Little Rock, Arkansas, and a woman came up to me and told me how her husband had left her after thirty years of marriage. She looked as if she were still shell-shocked. A woman from the Netherlands recently sent a message to my wife and told her that her ex-husband was divorcing his second wife, and that she would like to try and reconcile with him.

The marital dynamic is so important and can leave such devastation in its wake when people do not nurture this relational pillar. The wounds and casualties are deep and can take a lifetime to mend. With this in mind, again realize the wealth of skills and recourse our children will gain if we can find a way to endure the marital storms. Think of the plethora of examples they will have as they approach marriage, and realize that while God can do great things even if we have had difficult familial moments, the gift of a marriage grounded in selfless acts is one that will change the world.

That is what John Paul II is saying, and it is why the Church does so much to take the marital union seriously. When a marriage is working, we can see Christ as that lover who gave all things for his bride, the Church. When a marriage is working, people can see unconditional love in a couple that points them to God. Marriage is a structure that helps us become better people together than we would have been on our own, and that leads us to see possibilities in our relationship with God. On the other hand, a marital relationship that is falling apart will negatively impact our understanding of God's profound intimacy with us. We have been invited into the very life of the Trinity through baptism, and that intimacy with Christ and his bride is one that should be life giving. When a marriage is hurting, a relationship with Jesus can often be misunderstood and even hindered.

Marriage isn't the only foundational structure, though, that will help us to understand God better. The second relational pillar is friendship.

2. FRIENDS: POSSE, PEEPS, THUGS, AND THUGLETTS

There comes a time in most people's lives when they choose to tell all of their dreams and hopes, irritations and frustrations to their friends rather than to their parents. Recently I asked my teenage daughter if she liked any boys at school, to which she replied, "I'm not talking to you about that," to which I responded by asking her the question about a zillion more times.

(Anything to drive them a little crazy, right?) I understand this process of confiding less in parents and more in friends, though, and in many ways I am OK with the role of friendship. Having great friends can be one of the best things about our childhood, and as parents, hopefully we have instructed our children how to make wise friends before they select ones who can hinder rather than help their spiritual journey.

When I was a kid, my best friends were Brad and Brian. I think in every area of a child's life they were better than I was. They were smarter, did better in school and sports, were skinnier and more athletic, and from what I gathered by reasoned deduction, they were better-looking than I was. All the girls were interested in the twin boys, but apparently being friends with good-looking people doesn't necessarily mean you are as well. Life is so unfair! Over the years I wanted to be just like them. I tried to notch my belt on the same hole that they did, and as a result lost blood flow to my brain for most of my childhood. (It hasn't affected me at all!) We were inseparable, doing everything together. Hunting, building tunnels with hay bales, riding bikes, and camping are just some of the many things we did, which were always stuffed with fun moments and good memories. When it came to sports, they seemed to be built for success. When teams were chosen on the playground they were usually either picked to be team captains or were one of the first selected. Because they were my best friends, I would be picked quickly, even though I was slow and not very coordinated. Because they were my friends, I would try to do better on my tests and papers in school, striving to achieve excellence in an area that for them came naturally. How mathematics could be comprehended was a great mystery to me—and apparently still is, in that my checkbook continues to mock me with its inability to balance itself. When I was with my friends, I would play better basketball in our constant competitions against one another, and I would try things I normally wouldn't, like making fishing lures and reloading our shotgun shells after an afternoon of hunting. We regularly went hunting together, built forts, and made ninja throwing stars from the scrap metal lying about the farm. It was a great way to grow up and be a part of a family structure, especially since my own family wasn't able to remain intact. Friendship for me during these years was a place of stability and an opportunity to explore avenues I wouldn't have considered on my own.

Positive friendships can assist us in becoming better people. The support of our friends will aid us in being more holy, becoming better adults, and being well-rounded individuals who are stronger and more emotionally stable; these relationships can even aid in creative expression. True friendship is so important because in all areas we have one another's back and know that we are never alone.

Negative friendships, on the other hand, can lead us into areas that we would not have thought possible. The temptation to bow to peer pressure can be so great for young people—and for adults—that many find it impossible to be their true selves ever again. Lots of regret and pain can occur when we surround ourselves with negative friends. We are the way we are today, in part, because of those friendships and the peer pressure. As adults, we often feel regret when we think about our younger years, because we allowed ourselves to get caught up in so many things that seemed terribly important but in the end were just destructive, as we lost a bit of ourselves along the way.

During these years growing up in small-town America, I began to notice different ways in which my friends lived. A couple of my schoolmates had motorcycles, and seemed fearless as they rode around the country roads. There were friends of mine who were allowed to stay out late, had cool snacks that they could eat whenever they wanted, and regularly went out partying without any moral qualms whatsoever. One friend's father had the Playboy channel, and another's dad kept boxes of pornographic magazines in the basement. These friends opened up new avenues in which to lose myself, even though I'd been taught to run from such moral danger zones. Friendships were fostered and people often settled into various cliques that almost identified who they were becoming. There were the kids who would show up drunk to school, the athletes, the theater kids, and the band geeks. We had our cliques so that we could belong. Most people had a place to fit in with others, but there were always a few who seemed to wander about with little direction or support. Anything was better than having to be alone. God knows most of us would have easily settled into the drug-and-alcohol cliques rather than be one of the down-and-outs.

I remember a girl named Loretta, who was extremely awkward in a way that went beyond the typical middle-schooler. She looked odd, smelled funny, spoke and acted bizarrely, and for all intents and purposes fulfilled every possible requirement in the nerd category. I knew I wasn't supposed to make fun of her, but it was just so easy to do, and after all, most of my friends and fellow classmates didn't hold back their ridicule. I felt guilty because of the way we all spoke about her and to her, but whenever we attempted to be nice to Loretta she would respond in such odd and even confrontational ways. She would yell or respond to our jabs with sarcasm, anger filling her words and actions. She was alone. Over the years, technology has enabled most of us to connect through various social media outlets with almost anyone we ever knew and met in our earlier years. One day I asked a childhood friend who was coordinating school reunions whatever had happened to Loretta. If anyone would know, she would. She told me that she thought Loretta had died. I remember feeling so frustrated and even experiencing a sense of loss, wondering if Loretta had ever felt loved, whether she had ever mattered to someone, whether she'd ever had a real friend.

There are many girls like Loretta in our past, but there are many more in our present than we realize. One amazing way we can advocate for life is by cherishing each person who comes into our presence. A kind word to a stranger, a helping hand to those in need, and prayers for people who don't even realize they are in our intentions are all real ways to be pro-life. Let us witness to others the profound beauty of life by encountering Jesus in each person we meet. I think often our hurtful words to others when we are children stem from deep insecurity. We are afraid to befriend the outcast because we worry that by being in his or her presence, we ourselves are not far removed from such awkwardness. We do these same things as adults, but often we try and spin our poor behavior into something like justifiable concern. We all need friends, and this is something we are fit to be, even if those we meet are different from us.

Even though it would have been difficult during those early teen years, I do wish I could have found a better way to cherish the life of Loretta. In many ways I have been able to work on and foster some of these older relationships via social media, and for that I am thankful. Without this effort I wouldn't have known about an older friend's double mastectomy, another's constant feelings of insecurity and depression, or the many who have had failed marriages. Because of this interest in others I can cheer on a friend who has been freed from addiction to meth and alcohol. Friendship is worth the investment of our time and effort, and befriending people we aren't immediately drawn to is a worthwhile endeavor. Let's face it, after high school we begin to realize that the people we all thought were a little different are often the types of people we are eventually drawn to befriend. It is also true that the many folks we felt such a need to impress or imitate end up being terribly shallow as adults. When we leave those emotional teen years behind, there is such relief found in friendships that are not grounded in social cliques and fickle standards of popularity.

Our Church is meant to be a place where friendship is fostered. Regardless of our idiosyncratic ways, we should find acceptance there. Jesus encourages it. In fact, he says in John 15:13 and 14 that there isn't any greater love than when a man lays down his life for his friends, and we are his friends if we keep his commandments to love God and love others. When we find friendships that ground their actions in the self-donation expressed in the Gospel, we realize the power of a good companion. This type of love will impact who we are becoming and can help us in recovering from the person we were. Moments when superficial behavior, conditional friendship, and hurtful words are found in the Church are often the times many people leave it. We need friendship, and the place this relational gift should be vividly seen and experienced is in the Church.

A few years ago I was back in the Dakotas and had the chance to see the twin boys again, only now they were gigantic men. I hadn't seen them since we were about sixteen, but the moment Brad picked me up from the airport and we began to talk, it was almost as if no time had passed. We talked about jumping tires on our bikes and some of the good old days. Then Brad said he wanted to show me the house he had built with his own hands. I said sure, and then I thought how I'd love to show him my house, where my children were leaving applesauce containers all over the floor.

Brad's house was beautiful, and his new cars and Harley-Davidson affirmed what I had already suspected, that he was not struggling financially. I then went and saw his brother, Brian. What a glorious time we had catching up. As I was about to leave, Brian and I were talking in the driveway. I decided to tell him something I'd felt for a long time: "When we were young, I felt like I needed you guys way more than you needed me, but you were always cool with that." Brian responded, "Chris, you made everything we did so much better." I was very touched. Then he said something I wasn't prepared for: "You're doing exactly what we thought you'd be doing." I was baffled. After all my years of wanting to be like them, they truly saw something in me that I didn't see in myself. They remembered the funny stories I had told as a kid and saw how it had pressed out in the speaking I do around the world. They knew I was regularly involved in church and that faith was important to me, and saw how strong a role Christianity has in my work. The music I played in school, the plays and band I was involved in seemed to all be the beginnings of what I do now as I travel about sharing God's love through stories, music, and speaking. If you would have asked me as a young man, "What do you think you'll be doing as an adult?" I wouldn't have been able to answer with anything resembling what I do now. Actually, I would have said, "pig farmer," but that is another story. Even as teenagers, these two guys could see in me something that I didn't see in myself. Thank God for good friends.

What kind of friends do you have in your life? Are they the kind who lift you up, who see something in you that is amazing even when you doubt yourself? Do you have friends in your life who point you back to God's love even when you struggle with your faith? If not, ask God to bring you a great friend. If you have some wonderful people in your life who lift you up, thank God for such a blessing. Having good friends helps us to see and know the love Jesus has for us. Friendships that hurt and harm will hinder our understanding of God as friend. This is an important relational pillar God has given us so that we can come closer to him, but there is one other that we should carefully examine: the relationship with our significant other.

3. SIGNIFICANT OTHER

About a year ago I asked my 13 year old son, "Noah, when you are in the locker room with the football guys, do you ever talk about girls?" He looked at me like I was crazy and said, "Dad, why would we talk about girls when we can talk about something cool like football and video games?" Well, at least I had a couple of months remaining, it seemed, before I had to really start worrying about him. Later that year I asked him, "Noah, do you think any girls at school are interested in you? Do you think they like you?" Again, the exasperated look, which implied that I needed medical and psychological help, with the response, "Dad, how am I supposed to know what girls think?" In my mind I was thinking, If you can just keep that insight front and center in your thoughts, one day you will have a very successful marriage!

When I was in kindergarten I accidentally/on purpose kissed a little girl as we made our way down from our chairs to the floor for story time. Suddenly I was being made fun of by the rest of the class, and I quickly felt embarrassed. I realized that showing affection for someone I liked needed to be carefully pursued, so I fell in step with the traditional way of interacting with girls—and no, that didn't mean spitballs and pulling pigtails.

When we were young, the proper procedure to find out if our feelings were reciprocated was to write "the note." Remember the note? It involved a simple question written carefully on lined paper: "Do you like me? Check yes or no." And then, even before the creation of Excel documents and graphic options, there were two boxes that made the girl's response easily known to clueless boys across the country. As the little girls carefully unfolded our complex and unevenly folded secret messages, they methodically brought out their colored pencils, glitter, and for all I know even lip gloss and scribbled away their responses, putting hearts over the i's, adding unicorns and rainbows, and then folding the papers back up. When they came back to the senders, the tension was almost palpable. What did she write? Was she to be the one? The letters would be carefully opened, lips licked in anticipation, as the boys read the answer to this primal question. A check was carefully placed within a new box with the word: "maybe." Sigh! That wasn't an option, but at least there was a chance for true love. If only I'd had the wisdom my son has now, I could have avoided many years of sorrow!

In high school the relational procedure is different. You get your friends involved. The complexity of this in my day was such that if we would have put the energy into our schooling that we did in trying to find someone to date, we would have all been brilliant scientists (and you know how the girls love scientists!). As guys, we would talk about whom we liked, and then if one of our friends knew a friend of the girl being discussed, the friends would converse as true ambassadors and let the feelings be known, so that the female friend could eventually get the important information to the girl. It might seem complex, but it was fairly simple in that we didn't have to face immediate rejection. This may be an example of self-preservation, or even survival of the species. At some point, if given the green light— specifically, the girl didn't think you were a troglodyte—the awkward boy would make his way to the usually unnecessarily self-conscious girl, so that something amazing could take place: actually speaking face-to-face. With the guy dripping with Brut cologne and the girl sporting hair teased and sprayed into a work of art larger than a house (this was the '80s, with shoulder pads in a denim blouse, ensuring that her head wouldn't tilt too far to the left or right), this moment would bring them to a point of agreeing to meet at either the mall or possibly a movie theater. It is all so funny in retrospect, but it was terrifying in the moment. The awkward attempts at letting someone know you were interested in him or her were all worth it in the end if the person felt the same.

The realization that there might be someone out there beyond our family and friends who could relate to all of our erratic feelings, our dreams, and our desires was certainly primordial in its desire. Trying to find ways to make these relationships work could be clumsy and often impossible, but we tried and then tried again. What if we could find true love? What if we could find our soul mate? Heck, what if we could find someone who would actually go on a date with us?

With these relationships, there is a positive and negative dynamic, as we have seen with our relational structures of family and friends. A positive relationship with a significant other often shows young couples the benefits of being sacrificial and service oriented toward someone other than themselves. Caring about another took us outside our selfishness to a point of wanting to bring joy to the significant other, and the confidence of having pleased this special one we cared about was empowering. As young couples, we would save our money in order to buy one another gifts expressing our affection. We would sacrifice our family and time at work in order to be together, and often would try and find new ways of showing one another that there was no other who could make this world shine so bright. Was it idealistic and imperfect? Of course! But the desire to sacrifice so another can be blessed is very much a part of what it means to truly love. Wouldn't that be an amazing principle for married couples to remember?

If you think about it, often the goal in high school was to make enough money at work so that we could take our true love out to a movie and dinner. If we were really serious about it then there would be jewelry involved! We would beg parents, whom we usually ignored, for a few bucks so that we could spend it on the apple of our eye. It was a time of learning how to be generous and also a realization that in order to make something work we had to pay attention to one another. Often these relationships could be very selfless, but as most of us realized, a good thing could easily unravel after a short period of time.

The negative within these relationships emerged when we adopted selfishness, self-gratification, and a "using" mentality over and above selflessness and a serving mentality. The wounds from these negative relationships can be long lasting and deep. When we open our lives up to another with sincere vulnerability and then find that the relationship crumbles under selfishness, the rejection experienced by either person can bring emotional ramifications previously unimagined. I know a person who thought that everything was going amazing in her relationship, and she was even thinking about marriage options, when he informed her that he didn't want to be with her anymore. Talk to any kid in high school and they have a story of lost love, of being used and using others. So often, people hold to two different understandings of their relationship and what it is all about. The progression to simply hooking up, which we currently see in our high schools and colleges, is the fruition of people who have concluded that it is too much of a hassle to mess with long-term relational expectations and obligations. It is a "moment" mentality: Let's have a physical moment, and then not worry about trying to make something last, which we all know won't anyway. And for some reason, people have bought this relational approach! My thinking is that this was initiated more by men than by women.

Good dating relationships, engagements, and ultimately marriages point us to a deeper understanding of God's love for us. The selfless qualities in which we sacrifice and serve our true love are emphasized in the life of Jesus, especially in the cross. The more we work on a selfless love in these relationships, the easier it will be to have an understanding of just how much Christ demonstrated his love for us; and the more we look at the cross where Jesus showed his great love for us, the greater will be our love for the people we want to spend the rest of our lives with. Bad dating relationships, engagements, and marriages take away from our understanding of Jesus' love for us, his bride, the Church. Selfishness heaps greater misunderstanding upon the temporal reality of our relationships, and the way in which God loves us.

WRAP UP

Let's step back for a moment and reflect on our parental structure. The wounds from our parents can be so powerful and leave such a mark on our lives that often we stumble in our relationship with any type of father figure in religion. Sometimes the scars we carry are not even known until we begin to hear about a God who wishes to father us. For those who have had a great parental upbringing, the leap to seeing God as a benevolent father is not difficult at all.

Now remember the relational pillar of friendship. The friendships that have left so many wounds in our lives have certainly made us resistant to self-disclosure with others, and understandably so. Those experiences we have had with fair-weather friends can impact our willingness to be in community and certainly stifles holy vulnerability. If we have had great friendships, then I do think it is easier for us to befriend many whom we would never have interacted with in earlier days. Good friendships open us up to even more good friendships. Bad friendships close us off from the ones we have, and the ones we could have if we remained open. Good friendships point us to Jesus' friendship, and assist us in making that important relationship a deeper reality in our spirituality. Good friendships help us to identify the value and need for the saints who have gone before us, who long to assist us as true friends toward our final end.

And finally, as we have just discussed, the relationship with our significant other is an amazing stepping stone to a deeper comprehension of sacrifice and service, which should make it easier to be aware of Christ's love for us, his bride. When that relationship is hurtful and we use one another, the protective tendencies that are wired within each of us kick in, and we may close ourselves off to further pain. This lifestyle of self-preservation often means that we close ourselves off to authentic healing and future love. When a relationship is selfless and involves nurturing another toward greatness, we can find the intimacy offered and granted with Jesus as something truly life giving.

These primordial structures are either helping us know God and love him more, or they are giving us false insight and understanding of him, resulting in a coldness and greater distancing from anything that reminds us of our pain. Again, if your father was manipulative or abusive, you will likely find the invitation to know God as Father to be unappealing. In fact, it is likely that you will subconsciously distance yourself from that theological perspective. If your friends have betrayed your trust, it will be difficult to see Jesus as a friend who willingly sacrificed all for the relationship he chooses to foster with you. If your boyfriends and girlfriends have been one train wreck after another, seeing Jesus as the bridegroom or even the lover is an idea that you will likely run away from. Exploring these relational structures in this light can assist you in working toward healing and new beginnings. So don't give up, my friends, for I believe that the Lord is ready to father you if you have felt abandoned, encourage you if you feel betrayed, and embrace you if you have been rejected. God will never leave or forsake us, and Jesus promised to send a comforter, because his commitment to us is unwavering.

Take a few minutes and ask yourself how your relationships have impacted the way you look at Christianity. Is it possible many of the difficulties you have with the faith, which are likely justifiable, can be found to have originated in one of these three negative relational pillars? The amazing truth, or even better stated, the Good News, is that God wants you to know the beauty of his love as Father, even if your own father has been hurtful or absent. God wants you to experience the friendship found in Christ, even if your friendships have been stunted and fickle; and Jesus wants to invite you into unconditional love, even when you think of the messy past, or find yourself in conditional relationships today.

The hurt you have experienced is real, but Jesus' healing is greater and able to go beyond your negative experiences. The loneliness of abandonment is real, but Jesus wants you to know that he will never leave or forsake you. The regret you know so well is certainly crippling, but Jesus can forgive those sins, comfort you in your anxiety, and be a balm of soothing comfort and healing for your wounds. God will never force you to experience his love, but the invitation to know him and grow in that healing love is offered to you. Sometimes we have to remember that the hurt we have carried so long will need more than a quick cliché to bring about a proper perspective. Jesus is committed to loving you for as long as it takes. I love that truth. While we have often experienced conditional acceptance and love, God will always lovingly wait and willingly help us to know him. Be encouraged; there may be meaning to our life after all.

QUESTIONS

1. What were your parents like when you were younger? How did they process difficulties and celebrate victories?

2. Write down a list of the things your parents did well. See how God not only does those things for you but also goes beyond them. What stands out with this analysis?

3. Write down a list of the things your parents didn't do well. Ask God to fill in the gaps that were left in your life from this relationship.

4. Who were your best friends when you were younger? What about those relationships made you better, and what made you worse?

5. How can Christ be the friend you need right now?

6. What were the significant-other relationships you had growing up? How did you feel used? How did you feel empowered?

7. Can you see Christ as the most important relationship in your life? If not, what might need to change in your thinking?

FURTHER READING

In the matter of relationships, I would recommend the following books:

1. The Gospels. While this may seem to be a clichéd reference, the story of Jesus in the Bible should bring you a great sense of consolation.

2. *The Seven Levels of Intimacy*, by Matthew Kelly. This may be one of the best books on the importance of intimacy in our relationships.

CHAPTER 2:

IS THERE A MEANING TO OUR LIFE?

Is there a universal meaning to all life? Or is the life we live relative? This is a very important question I think we need to address before going much further. Many may think I am reading way too much into relational pillars, but we can all conclude that even if they aren't overtly showing us a grander picture of God, those relationships have impacted who we have become. The question at hand is not important for us just today, but has been for all ages. The meaning of life is of such significance that Monty Python addressed it—now, that's serious!

Here is one thing that we can likely agree upon: Most of the world's populace could easily be categorized as religious beings (see CCC 26, 27). The majority of religious expressions from the past and present all state the obvious: We didn't just accidentally arrive here on this planet. There must be a maker, or at least an all-powerful being, because the complexity of the created order is too great to simply pass over as accidental. We want to know there is someone or something that is ultimately in control, and religion tries to answer that in a variety of ways (see *Nostra Aetate*). Some religions are polytheistic, and the actions of the deities are often tied in various ways to what an individual does or does not do. Even people who are primarily agnostic acknowledge that there is some type of creative being, albeit one that is not clearly known. Those who posit an atheistic viewpoint may be growing in number or at least visibility, but it is still an ideology that is held by very few. Why? Because the human person wants meaning instead of meaninglessness, and religion gives us some pillars that ensure life is valued. Even atheists have a basic ethic of life. "What is it that I ought or ought not do?" is a question that each individual, whether holding to a structured religious ideology or not, faces in a variety of moral scenarios. The universal question of life having purpose and meaning is proof positive that there is at least a god of some type. Simply put, who cares what we do or don't do if we are randomly placed here for a brief period of time?

The human person is conditioned to ask questions of great significance. The Catholic Church says in Vatican II's *Nostra Aetate* that religion answers these universal questions of Who am I and Why am I here. One of the wonderful things about the Catholic Church is that it typically isn't afraid of artistic expression, appreciation of beauty, the pursuit of truth, and the longing for goodness. Some great Christian minds have willingly gone toe-to-toe with very complex questions because the God they served was greater than our deepest thoughts. There have been horrible times in the Church's history when the arts have been hindered and individual expressions of faith have been battled, but overall, the Church recognizes that we need answers. Catholics evangelize, as do many religions, because we believe that we have the most satisfying answers to these primordial questions.

Christianity is unique in the grand scheme of religions, not because it is the only system that has a religious leader worthy of emulation, nor because it is the only religion that has philosophical tenets that help us become generous people, law-abiding citizens, and good mothers and fathers. Christianity is revolutionary because it shows us a way to live that is beyond the world's greatest expectations, and because the founder, Jesus Christ, rose from the dead to offer us something that no one could ever have offered in and of themselves: forgiveness for the great offense of original and even actual sin. While many outside the Christian Church don't use words like *sin*, they do understand the disordered manifestations of the human condition. You don't have to be a Christian to recognize that murder is intrinsically disordered, that Hitler held and posited ideals that destroyed innocent lives, that lying and using one another is not what the human person should be about. Christianity does tell us why these qualities are disordered and why they are out of step with what the human experience should be. The faith not only tells us why things are not appropriate, but it also gives to us a way we can live that is beyond instinctual living.

I have an amazing English bulldog named Hagrid. He's a wizard; he wizzes all over the house! This dog is so ugly he is cute—and luckily so, because the naughtiness of this dog could rival that of the worst criminals in our juvenile facilities. He steals food, potties in areas that are not appropriate, speaks out of turn, and tries to mate with anything that moves. He is a glutton and a lustful creature, but we understand that in some way this is part of what a dog is like. Even still, we try and train him so that he goes to the bathroom outside and doesn't steal the baby's peanut butter sandwich, and we reprimand him when he confuses our legs for another dog. If we as humans just gave in to every urge and instinct as if we were only animals, we would all be either in jail, morbidly obese, or completely unproductive due to a slothlike lifestyle.

Christianity speaks to the heart of the matter, which is that the human person is created by a God that knows all and has intentionally chosen for us to be in time here and now. Christianity is about this God becoming flesh and dwelling among us, and Jesus doesn't just speak about what our human condition should be, but he shows us how to live a life in loving obedience to a father God who has always been actively interested in those he created. Christianity is not just a religion of tolerance; it is also a relationship in which people begin to finally see what greatness the human person is truly called to and is capable of.

Often we become sidetracked by the crazy characters who speak about Christianity, or even the historical moments when the faith was hindered due to wretched leaders, and we somehow conclude that this is the norm. Jesus himself showed us that just because someone speaks about him doesn't mean that person is truly following this heroic way of life. Think about Judas for a moment and you will see what I mean. Jesus said that there would be weeds with the wheat, and really, our job is not to point out which of the two a person is; instead, it is to do our best to water the seed when we can, lest in our zeal we uproot one of the wheat stalks. If Christianity is more about a relationship with Christ, who shows us how to live, then it means we should find out what Jesus revealed to us when he lived among us.

The four Gospels are the account of Jesus' life, death, burial, and Resurrection. They speak about Christ in a variety of ways, because each of the authors found the life of Jesus so profoundly applicable to the audiences for which they wrote. When you gather the material about Christ together you realize that his love for all, including the Pharisees, is something that we as human persons recognize as intrinsically good. Even people of other faiths find the life of Christ worthy of meditation and appreciation, which is why so many consider him a wonderful teacher and prophet. Jesus not only cared for the people who were considered worthless during his time, such as the tax collectors, the woman caught in the act of adultery, and the Samaritan woman, but he told stories that emphasized the need for us to truly love and forgive one another. He told us to forgive seventy times seven, to serve rather than to be served, and to be like the Good Samaritan, who didn't ignore the battered individual so many had passed along the way.

What we realize from these written accounts is that Jesus didn't do these things so that we could just have another hero to look up to; he did these things to be obedient to the Father and show us there is meaning in this life. He demonstrated to us that we were made to be in a relationship with God, whom we can call Abba, or Daddy. This revelation of what a relationship with God can be like is so unique that we can truly say it is the singular universal truth amid the religious milieu throughout all of time. Certainly there have been stories of mythological gods interacting with humans, but Jesus doesn't initiate a relationship with us so that we can be manipulated into doing the will of an angry deity; rather, he offers a relationship with us so that we can be the most joy-filled, purpose-driven human persons he created us to be. We are now invited by Jesus himself into this intimate relationship, and it is our choice to accept or decline.

Later on in the New Testament, Saint Paul talks about the intimacy Jesus has with us, his Church. He uses images that we can relate to, like a body or a marriage. Paul says that Christ is the head and we are the body, and this unity is of such profundity that we must all truly work together in order to live life abundantly. The love Jesus has for us is bridal, says Paul, in that he truly gives himself to us so completely that it is life giving. Even in the Gospels we have a picture of this type of relationship, when we read, "I am the vine, you are the branches." (John 15:5)

If we have a God who truly does love us, enough to walk among us and show us what this type of relationship can look like, then we should have a greater peace about giving our lives to him. If Jesus is God in the flesh, and has the power to take our broken past and set it aright, then we can trust that he is going to bring us to a greatness of living that can honestly be termed "abundant life." I want this Christianity! I want to know a Jesus who encounters me in my mess and is not afraid to love me. I want to follow an individual who will forgive me the countless times I fail him, and I believe that is something that you want too. Jesus Christ still asks us the very question we remember him asking the disciples so long ago: "Who do you say that I am?" (Mark 8:29) If we conclude that he is only a good man, then we will not be able to fathom the lives of the saints, who experienced insane obstacles and yet left a witness of heroic virtue. If we can only see Jesus as a sage whose life was tragically cut short, then we will miss out on the gift of forgiveness that he gave when he victoriously rose from the dead. Most of us realize Jesus is more than a wise man and greater than a good man. You are likely way past those ideas, but your questions about Christ are just as important for your growing spirituality. Is Jesus waiting with his iron fist, ready to judge us? Or is he watching from a distance, uninterested, or even capable of really solving the problems we are facing in our lives? How do we guarantee his involvement?

While most consider Jesus an important man, wise and good, and likely greater than we realize, when it is all said and done we want to know if Jesus is able to help us in our lives, and if he is able, is he willing? When Jesus sees that we are not OK, does he really want to love us even before we are capable of changing? I want to encourage you, so remember the previous examples of the tax collector, the adulterer, the Good Samaritan, and the Samaritan woman, because Jesus becomes present for each of you as he was for them. Will you let him heal your desire for false security, or will you continue to trust in the world's obsession of wealth? Will you try to drown your insecurities or mistakes in false relational paths or acts of self-gratification, or will you allow Jesus to truly see and love you? Will you acknowledge that you are beaten and ignored by so many, but that you have a chance to be cared for and healed in Christ? And will you let Jesus speak to the deep, secret places in your heart, and see that he is not rejecting you for all your past mistakes, that instead he is offering you a new opportunity to drink from the well of water that is living and without end?

You see, I believe there truly is meaning for us in this life, and that meaning rests in the call that Jesus gave so long ago: "Come unto me all you who are weak and heavy laden and I will give you rest." (Matthew 11:28) Jesus loves you and me enough that he will allow us to simply consider him a good teacher from days gone by. He will not force us to serve or follow him as the disciples chose to do, nor will he make us kneel in worship as the Wise Men did in the infancy narratives. Jesus will not make us give our allegiance to him, because what he is asking for is a free response that ultimately only we can make. He is inviting us into a relationship. Will you believe that Jesus is love incarnate? Will you believe that he wants to love you right where you are, in order to envelop you and give you a purpose in life? The Scriptures even say, "While we were yet sinners Christ died for us." (Romans 5:8) In other words, he isn't waiting for you to be perfect before he accepts you. Jesus looks at you battered by the world and the failings you've experienced thus far and is your Good Samaritan.

It is my intention throughout this book to remind you of this Jesus who embodies goodness, because I am afraid that we have believed many false ideas of what he is like. If you believe that Jesus is just a wise man, or only a mystic, then you will not freely give your life to him. Following Christ truly gives us purpose in this life, and while things can be very difficult, he is with us in a way that genuinely matters. Even if the storms we encounter are overwhelming, Jesus walks upon the sea and finds us in our need. This is the Jesus I am speaking about, and this is the person I am growing in a relationship with. The reasons for our struggles in accepting Jesus are many, and in the next chapter I hope to address a few of those so that we can find clarity amid life's confusion.

A little while ago I heard a famous theologian speak about an encounter he'd had with a college student who had great difficulty with Christianity. For a lengthy period of time the man listened to the rant and complaints of this young student as he articulated the many problems he had with the faith. In the end, the theologian said, he completely agreed with everything the student had stated and was just as angry. The young man was baffled. "How can you remain a follower of Christ, then, if you agree with all that I have stated?" The theologian said, "The Jesus I know is nothing like the Jesus you've been talking about." I think this is very much where many find themselves today. I hope you will give Christ another chance, because you would be amazed to find out that I am just as angry and frustrated as you are about the many ways people have poorly witnessed the Christian faith throughout the years.

What is your purpose in life? If we simply see that humanity as a whole longs for answers to deeper questions and attempts to address this longing with the constructs of religion, we can at least be sympathetic to one another's desire for meaning. If we can see Jesus as unique among all the religious leaders, which he posits that he is (the way, the truth, the life), then we have to make a choice: Is Jesus who he says he is? If our conclusion is yes, then we have a whole new way of addressing life's obstacles, and a true purpose: to be loved and to love others. What is your purpose in life? It is to know God's love for you, so that you will freely choose to serve and honor him in this life, in order to spend eternity with him in the next. I believe this with all my heart, and it has impacted the way I live my life. My purpose is to be in a relationship with God, who has done all things to help that purpose to come to fruition. He has done this for you as well. Do you want to have a relationship with God? He certainly has done everything to have a relationship with you. I wonder if you will step deeper into the mystery of God's love. Who do you say Jesus is?

QUESTIONS

1. What examples do we have that show how the human person is a religious being?

2. What role does religion play in the human experience? What things can you consider different about Christianity?

3. How does our understanding of Jesus impact the way we deal with our circumstances and spirituality?

4. What is your purpose in life? Can you see how Jesus can bring to fruition the purpose you have been given by God?

FURTHER READING

1. *Catechism of the Catholic Church #26–#184*

2. *Nostra Aetate, Vatican II*

3. *Mere Christianity,* by C. S. Lewis

CHAPTER 3:
THE WOUND:
WE ARE ALL BROKEN

THE PROBLEM

There is an eight-hundred-pound gorilla in the room that most people refuse to acknowledge, which generally is the case when it comes to eight-hundred-pound gorillas. In this circumstance, this unaddressed monstrosity is the fact that we are all wounded. We all have an ugly part of our lives that we'd rather not make known to others. While most of us don't want to talk about this universal reality of our past wounds, it is something we are all aware of to varying degrees. We will talk about these past wounds in a moment, but there is another wounded part of each person that is usually not specifically tied to something we have done. It is a wound that we are all born with. I am not speaking about a physical quality that we can readily point to in one another; rather, I am talking about our brokenness, which is within each and every one of us from our birth. What is the specific problem? It is the impact and effect of what is called "original sin." I am speaking as a Christian, but people of all faiths and walks of life can detect this wound in one way or another. For the Christian, the wound is the result of a deep and lasting act of disobedience that we call sin; for the world, it is the problem of evil, which for some is explained by an individual's selfishness or being born with "loose wiring." Let me explain this a bit from a Christian point of view, and then I will address it from a more general understanding. This chapter is primarily a foundation for us to reveal the wounds we carry and the ways we often try to cope with them.

Christianity teaches about original sin, a reality that impacts each individual. This wound originates in the first couple, Adam and Eve. In the Genesis account, the primordial couple makes a choice to directly disobey their Creator. There is one tree within the Garden of Eden they are told to avoid, the Tree of the Knowledge of Good and Evil, and from all others they are allowed to partake. One could easily ask, Why avoid this tree at all if in fact it will give knowledge of good and evil to those who consume its fruit? Maybe an even more pointed question would be, God, why have such a tree placed in this Garden of Eden in the first place? The answer is probably simpler than one would initially think. The tree is there so that Adam and Eve can freely respond to their Creator with either obedience or disobedience. Love, if it is of any merit and authenticity, must have an option for each participant to willingly choose a path in favor of the other's request or in contradiction of it. This ability to choose differentiates us from nonrational creations, as well as establishes the possibility in this context of a unique relationship with our maker. To be able to obey and even to disobey are the necessary qualities in which a framework of love can best function. If in this primitive story the couple chooses to avoid the tree that their Creator commands they stay away from, their act proves that they are willing to submit out of love to the wishes of the person making the request. But if the couple chooses to disobey, it in fact proves that there is a lack of trust in God's goodness, and a willingness to differentiate themselves as independent from the one who makes such a command. Adam and Eve are invited into such a unique relationship with their Creator, vividly exemplified in this opportunity to choose either obedience or disobedience. This act of disobedience demonstrates the couple's lack of trust in the benevolence of God. The choice of Adam and Eve to disobey had numerous effects, and while we know the consequences of their disobedience, we can only imagine what would have happened if the two had set themselves freely upon the path in which they obeyed their Creator's command.

The communion the first couple has with God is without tension between their will and emotions, and they are able to live in this state without the threat of mortality. The human body over time will certainly die, but in the Garden of Eden we see death is a consequence of disobedience; therefore, for a period of time Adam and Eve naturally age but do not undergo any decay and demise in the flesh. The first couple are also at peace with themselves individually as well as together. Their physical needs are met with the abundance of food, and the responsibilities and tasks given to Adam to tend and protect what has been entrusted to him bring him genuine satisfaction for doing them freely. The disobedience of this couple brings about their mortality, the loss of integrity between their will and emotions, and a lack of unity with God, self, and others. Because they represent all of humanity (*Adam* means "man"), their progeny will receive the stain of original sin. We know from the Genesis account that the couple is removed from the Garden of Eden and will now have to work by the sweat of their brows to till the soil in order to enjoy the fruits of their labor, which in Eden was dangling within arm's reach from every tree. Banished from the garden, the woman will experience painful labor in childbirth and the tension between man and woman will be emphasized in her wanting control over him. This story is called "the fall," because not only did they disobey God, but they also lost the relationship's fruitfulness for which they were created. We can easily ask why their choices impact us today, but even in a basic understanding of life, if I chose to commit a crime such as murder, my life, the lives of those who depend upon me, and the victim's life would all be impacted forever. Choices that we make don't only impact each one of us, but they have a ripple effect, touching more people than we could have ever imagined. The classic Christmas movie *It's a Wonderful Life* illustrates this cause-and-effect with cinematic brilliance.

What could Adam and Eve's life have looked like if they had chosen to submit to the authority of their Creator? What if they had avoided the Tree of the Knowledge of Good and Evil? We could conclude that the story we are about to tell would have been radically different, although the specifics of such an outcome remain a bit ambiguous. What is clear from the given story is that a period of testing or probation was necessary even in this place of peace, so that the couple could choose to either obey or disobey. Again, love must be something freely chosen.

Obedience is done willingly when love is the foundation of a person's actions.

When Eve is tempted in the Garden of Eden, with Adam saying and doing nothing to defend and protect that which he was given (his helpmate), the period of probation comes to a mortal conclusion. Adam was the priest within the garden and he could have brought Eve closer to God. He was also the prophet in this context, and he absolutely should have reaffirmed and articulated to Eve God's command to obey his will. Adam was also the king in this setting, given responsibilities to ensure the safety and care of the garden. If he would have defended his bride from the serpent, even to the point of laying down his life, or simply directed her away from the tree in the first place, it is possible that the two would have encountered a battle with the serpent nonetheless, but the act of fighting to obey God's command would have demonstrated success in this period of probation. Maybe the act of fighting for his bride would have resulted in Adam and Eve going to partake in the Tree of Life, or if slain by the serpent they would have been raised to life by God, who was found walking in the garden right after the fall. What could have happened if Adam had obeyed? Possibly the second person of the Blessed Trinity would have come to fight on their behalf, since they would have proven their willingness to obey God even if they were to die upholding his command.

This drama in the garden is a very important story that many have quickly dismissed. While it is a story of origins and can easily fall in step with mythic literature, we realize that the importance of this account is greater than first imagined, based on Jesus' death, burial, and Resurrection. Jesus allows us to view the Old Testament stories through a different lens, and in this case we begin to see that our need for salvation is much greater than we might have realized. The Scriptures are inspired, which means God breathed, and in fact, *Dei Verbum*, a document from Vatican II on divine revelation, says that God is the primary author of Sacred Scripture. So what does this mean for us? It means there is a rhyme and reason to this story that impacts our eternal destiny.

Some may ask, Why make such radical leaps from such a simple tale? Why apply anything to our lives today from such an ancient mythic creation account? As Christians, we know that the Bible isn't just a book with interesting stories. The Church will say that not only is God the primary author of Scripture, but the accounts are given for our salvation.

The story of Adam and Eve is one that is very important for us today, and we can see this in Saint Paul's writings. He calls Jesus the Last Adam, and for us to understand how Jesus' one act of obedience to the Father can impact all of mankind, we should know that the one act of the first man, Adam, had a negative impact upon all of mankind. Simply look at Jesus, the Last Adam (1 Corinthians 15:45), and see that he obeys the will of his father, even when he is tempted to meet his own needs in his own ways, and he fights for his bride, even to the death.

Jesus battles the serpent of old, not only in the temptations in the wilderness, but as he is led to the cross. There upon a wooden beam, Jesus is crucified at Calvary, Golgotha, the Place of the Skull, and this period of testing brings about a radically different end to an otherwise dismal tale of human existence. Jesus, as the ultimate man, willingly follows and obeys the words of the Father, and not the tempting hiss of the serpent. Jesus, as a man willing to tend and keep, protect and honor all that he has been given, as Adam was instructed to do, shows what love looks like in time: obedience. Jesus as the priest makes an everlasting sacrifice to the Father, as the prophet speaks clearly the word of the Lord, and as the king, he invites us into the Kingdom of God. The wound of sin, along with its ramifications, is within us all, but the healing Christ gives can be received by all who wish to align themselves again with the will of God.

This is all pretty amazing stuff, and in fact, the consequences of this story can bring a sense of real joy and peace, even if our brows are beaded with sweat from our labors. Real peace can be within each of us as we face struggles between our will and our emotions. The rest of what we long for is actualized in the gift of love Jesus gives, even when life's difficulties seem overwhelming. What the wound within each human person reminds us of is that we are in need of a savior. Adam should have been a savior to Eve, but he wasn't. Jesus was a savior to the world, but even this act will not be forced upon anyone. The salvific work of Christ is freely offered to you, because you cannot remedy on your own what was done by Adam and Eve. You need a hero, someone who will fight to the death for you, regardless of the foe. Jesus comes and gives to us the fruit of life from the Tree of Life by his death, burial, and Resurrection. He is the valiant knight, the epic hero king, the groom defending his bride against harm. This is why Christianity spends so much time talking about Jesus, because he gives to us truly good news: salvation and healing from our wound.

The world doesn't really use this language, but let's speak in some general and universal terms so that we can make this very practical. People are religious beings. When we look at the history of the human race, we can see so many variations of worship within the constructs of our culture. From the ancient Near Eastern religions and uncivilized primitive races to the monotheistic religions, there are a multitude of religions constructed to calm the hearts of people who realize that there must be something more to life than just self-gratification. The consequences for those who follow these religious principles enable individuals to settle into their humanity with a little more familiarity. Even for those who have religious or philosophical tenets very much at odds with Christianity, there is a basic ethic to life of what an individual ought or ought not do. Simply put, even in a tribal situation, a member of the tribe could not go into the chief's tent and be with his wife without a severe consequence, which likely would be death. Why? Because the human person recognizes that there is a need for order and structure, for answers to deep primordial questions, for an individual and collective purpose. All religions and even individual efforts function better with these answers and emphasized purposes.

The question of ethics is a pretty important one, and it can be argued that all individuals must deal with a basic ethic of life, because it is part of being human. Why is there evil in the world? Why do bad things happen to good people? These are deep questions all people have wrestled with in this journey called life, and religion helps to answer those questions.

There is a sea of people who may have had religious influences from earlier, formative years, but within this age of reason and technology, it seems a common tendency to rid ourselves of the restrictions of all that is old and embrace what feels good or gives us an exciting purpose. Why worry about the confines of an outdated religion? We are advanced and have evolved to a point where we can move beyond superstition and myth. With all this human advancement and a tendency to look down upon previously uneducated generations, there is still a problem of evil and moral failings within the heart of men. For the intellectual who has no place for religion in his life, the problem of evil or moral failings can often be whittled down to a propensity toward selfish behavior with no regard for those in his community. For some, the evil demonstrated is simply an occasional blip in the genetic makeup of an individual who was faulty from the start. I am sure some have felt that societal or familial abuses and dysfunction have produced such evil, but in the end we must acknowledge that there are many unfortunate examples of people who are not living life in a way that benefits themselves or others.

While Christianity has seen its fair share of difficult times, the matter at hand is our wounded existence. All people—past, present, and future—wrestle with individual choices, which can hurt others, and the impact of choices made by others, which can change our lives for better or worse. This reality of an ability to destroy another's dreams and even life is beyond a religion's or even a region's primary ethical structure. It is a problem addressed in all cultures and even in the religious tenets of faith. For the Jewish people, "Thou shalt not kill" (Exodus 20:13) is still applicable today, as it is for Christians. Murder is something that advanced cultures do not tolerate, even if they stand at odds with the confines of a monotheistic religion such as Judaism.

Why can't we all just get along? Because we make a choice to do something that will either enhance the community or disturb it. We will either see ourselves as an island and do whatever we wish, or we will recognize that we are part of a village. These are very common themes that have been raised in cinema and written accounts because they are truths connecting us globally. There are some basic responses the human person has when she is confronted with the power of her choice to enhance or harm. When an individual realizes that she is capable of hurting another with her words, it can either cause her to be more careful in what she says, or she may brashly move forward in hurting another nonetheless. In order to protect ourselves from being harmed by others, or from being ruled by the past, which has already hurt us, we often resort to these three self-preserving responses: We build walls, wear masks, or bury the pain. For the individual who sees the value of using her choice to enhance those around her, greatness becomes evident in a multitude of ways. Let's examine the avenues that we regularly use to deal with actions of harm so that we can find ways to understand where we have been and where we will go.

QUESTIONS

1. How does Christianity acknowledge the problem of evil?

2. Why did Adam and Eve sin? How does Christ counter this sin as the Last Adam?

3. What can we say about a society's understanding of basic ethics (what one ought or ought not do)?

4. How might a non-Christian answer the question of evil or immoral behavior?

5. The impact that we have upon others can be life-changing. Can you think of people who have harmed you with their words or actions? Have you said or done things that hurt others?

6. Is there hope or an answer to evil?

FURTHER READING

1. The book of Genesis

2. *First Comes Love: Finding Your Family in the Church and the Trinity* by Scott Hahn

3. *It's a Wonderful Life* (movie)

CHAPTER 4:
SELF-PRESERVATION

Most of us were probably told when we were young, "If you can't say something nice, don't say anything at all." That principle seemed universal in the places I grew up, and I am guessing you've heard it as well. There is another expression I bet we could quote: "Sticks and stones may break my bones, but words will never hurt me." While that seems ideal, anyone who has had someone speak poorly of him or others knows full well that those words can leave scars and lasting wounds more hurtful than those from a rock or stick.

While the human condition may be flawed because of sin, there is an important theme at work here: Words matter. Jesus himself spoke about the power of the tongue, and if you think about your own life, I bet you can remember with unfortunate vividness the sting of another's words to you. I remember visiting my father overseas when I was a teen. We were talking about religion and politics, and at one point in the dialogue my father looked at me and said, "Chris, you stand for everything that I hate." I went up to my room feeling crushed, realizing that I was unable to gain my father's approval. I spent some time crying that afternoon and tried to gather my wits about me in order to head down for dinner. Many years later my father and I spent some time together at my home. He was visiting, and as was our habit, we began talking about life, family, and eventually politics and religion. In the middle of the conversation I was thinking that my father stood for so many moral issues that I felt strongly opposed to. While I didn't articulate it, I realized a bit more clearly the frustration my father must have felt as he viewed my mother's influence in my life when I was a young man, probably wishing that he could have been more involved in my philosophical formation. We have worked through a lot of our inability to communicate, and I cherish his friendship, but those were some difficult years for both of us.

When we find ourselves hurt by another's actions or words, we often do a few things to ensure self-preservation. To adjust to the selfish actions of others toward us, we build walls, wear masks, and often bury our feelings so that we can survive this thing called life.

WALLS

When I think of walls I think of old castles. It is pretty incredible to behold the ingenuity of earlier civilized peoples. The moat surrounding these massive walls would ensure the protection of the castle's inhabitants. Generally walls are built to keep those within safe from those without who would willingly plunder all that is within. I believe we instinctively build emotional walls in order to protect ourselves from those who have hurt us before. The classic account of the Trojan horse is especially applicable in terms of people who we thought cared for us but who actually came into our inner selves and harmed us rather than built us up. I wonder if the many walls we construct are simply an attempt to build ourselves up when we know that many are trying to break us down. These walls can be very strong in our lives, depending upon the opposing forces. People who have been hurt by those they should have been able to trust often take a long time to let others into their lives again. Whether it is from emotional, physical, or psychological abuses, our walls unfortunately keep us enclosed as well as keep others at a safe distance.

What walls are in your life? Many may say that they haven't had great tragedies befall them and therefore there are no walls to be deconstructed, and yet often from the earliest days we learn that self-preservation isn't an accident. Think of when you were young and someone made fun of the way you dressed or talked. Kids can certainly be cruel, and it is often during the younger years that we quickly construct ways to cope with these moments of pain. I used humor to deflect hurtful words. If I could make people laugh, or point other people's attention to someone even weaker than I was, I knew that I would be safer from the jeers of my classmates. This is not a small matter, and I believe an expression from my wife fits very well here: "Hurt people say hurtful things." We don't usually consider the fact that the bully is likely the way he is due to the hurtful events in his own life, but this is so often the case. As adults we are still in the business of building walls. Unfortunately, we encounter people who regularly hurt us with their actions and words. We shut ourselves off from these individuals to avoid further wounds.

We decline invitations to gatherings with people who hurt us in order to avoid the possibility of further pain. We often adopt a persona that lets others know we are not to be trifled with. We hide behind our clothes, our inflated spirituality, money, intellect, and education, all in the name of self-preservation. We avoid anything that could be a confrontation. While I suggest avoiding people who break us down emotionally, I think we need to try and get a handle on why these areas strike us so deeply. In the end, wouldn't it be nice if we could honestly be ourselves and not have to worry about being damaged? It seems like wishful thinking in our day and age, and yet I do believe it is possible to live in a way that is stronger than a life behind walls. What I propose is a life soaked in love, but before unpacking this, we have to look at another aspect of self-preservation: the masks we wear.

MASKS

Dressing up for Halloween can be a very fun experience for children because they can pretend to be something or someone that they are not. My mother made a Batman costume for me one Halloween. I was so excited that I could hardly wait to go out collecting candy with her. I fell asleep that afternoon, and when I awoke it was evening. Panicked, I jumped out of bed with my heart racing: I'd missed Halloween! I scurried to get my Batman outfit and jumped into it as fast as possible, running to my mother, only to find out that Halloween wasn't until the next evening. I was disoriented and relieved.

For adults there are large gatherings and parties where each person wears a mask, and part of the fun can be trying to find those friends of ours who have hidden themselves behind masterful costumes. These parties are entertaining, but we know Monday demands we remove our masks and return to the real world and the regularity that awaits us.

While Halloween masks are visible, the masks I am talking about are unseen by most, which is actually proof that we are successful in our deception. Our ultimate goal is to avoid revealing the reality of what lies behind the mask, the reality of our mess. The cliché "If only you really knew me" is strong at work here. We have a certain mask in our workplaces, and another set of masks we wear for the strangers we encounter, the neighbors we wave to, and the fellow parish members we are surrounded by in church. For example, when we go to check out at the grocery store, inevitably we hear, "How are you today?" We all know that the cashier has no real interest in our lives, our problems and worries, so we respond with, "Great." Even though everything isn't, in fact, great, the mask is in place and we don't have to talk about anything of importance.

I remember as a kid feeling like everyone at my church knew my parents were divorced and not wanting to talk about it. In fact, if any teacher or minister were to try and sympathize with my loneliness, I would quickly brush it off and try to avoid any type of dialogue about this more painful part of my life. The mask was meant to help me avoid the questions of people pretending to care, or even keep others at bay who actually did care.

I believe we learn how to put on masks at an early age. When I was young we had a reading incentive in school. For each book we read we could put a star on a paper flag we had made. The flags were stapled to the walls and we could all see how many books each child had read throughout the year. There was a girl in class named Beth, who was not only reading many books, but most of them didn't even have pictures! Good grief. I went home and tried to find every children's book I could and read them as fast as possible so that I could have more stars on my flag than Beth. Some of my friends were reading the Hardy Boys and I struggled with finishing the Berenstain Bears. I certainly didn't want to come off as childish, so I would just quietly nod and pretend I knew how good those Hardy Boys mysteries were. It seems awfully silly to worry about how many books one can read in a year, but for me, it was a very important task, and I didn't want others to think I wasn't smart.

We practically instruct each other how to pretend we are better than we really are at certain activities, and if we have our masks on right we can certainly trick a lot of people. Why do we have a mask readily in place when someone we know tries to care for us? Recently my neighbor suffered a miscarriage, but the day after she got out of the hospital she ran a community event with no one the wiser. The last thing she wanted was for anyone to notice the pain she was experiencing. Another individual I know had an abortion in her youth, and I have not once heard her talk about the child or the forgiveness the Lord has given her. She is very outspoken about how God has changed her life, but this topic remains hidden. We want people to think we are who we are pretending to be. We want people to think that the way they have hurt us is something that easily rolled off us, like water from a duck's back. Look at the lyrics to a Taylor Swift song called "I'm Alright": *But now that we said good-bye I'll pretend that I'm alright yeah, I'm alright, I'm alright. You said you didn't wanna see me cry but I'll pretend that I'm alright, I'm alright, I'm alright.*

What if we could actually be loved for who we are, mistakes and all? If you were to think about the various ways you wear masks, I am sure most would consider them an understandable reality, if not a necessity. While I think wearing masks is a common tactic that we all use either knowingly or unknowingly, the opportunity to live free and be truly ourselves is an ideal worth exploring.

BURY IT

The third way we ensure self-preservation is by burying the pain and difficulty of the past. This suppression of hurt feelings and our previous painful experiences can be easily done through entertainment, drugs, sex, alcohol, or any number of other agents of distraction. If we can get into the rhythm of noise and stay there, we can avoid the whispers from our past waiting in the silence. I am certainly not talking about a constant state of introspection, but let's be honest—we do what we can to keep ourselves busy.

Silence is an awfully powerful reality. For many, it is so disarming that they have attempted to fill every moment with some kind of noise. We are often afraid of silence. Maybe this fear is fueled by an even greater fear of being rejected, or maybe we think that we are simply too weak to deal with what may resurface in the quiet; regardless, we need to deal with our issues, not ignore them. If we occasionally allow for quiet, we realize that need to address the pain of our lives. In the silence, we can often hear Christ speaking the healing words we need most. Sometimes this is too painful for us to address head-on, and so, rather than invite Christ into this pain, we bury it deeper and deeper.

So many look for comfort in food, but they remain hungry for love and acceptance, while other people may bury pain with the pursuit of money, thinking that it will solve all their problems. We try and bury our wounds in frivolous activities, under fear and anger, but the pain remains. There isn't a drug that can numb us enough to take away this pain, but so often it is a path chosen by those desperate to forget. Jesus' love for us is steady and continues when we often flee. While this defensive quality is understandable, intentionally avoiding the wounds from our own actions and from others' toward us never brings about the healing we desperately crave. Jesus wants us to be healed even more than we do. He knows that we will not be happy drowning our pain in alcohol, so he quietly invites us not to forget our struggle, but to lay it at his nail-scarred feet.

We are in need of healing, and interestingly enough we are not only the recipients of this healing from Jesus Christ but also the potential agents for others' journeys to victory.

RECIPIENT

While many of our past wounds are not forgotten, often their pain can be alleviated with the balm of an apology or reconciliation. As the recipients of this healing, we can continue forward with life a lot more easily. The power of our words is amazing, and when others use their words as agents of healing, we can move on from the rut in the road that has held us up for so long.

Recently while my wife was riding her bike on her favorite trail, she arrived at a portion that was blocked by a fallen tree. The tree was too heavy for her to move, so she had to find a new route. Later that day as she came near the blocked path again, she noticed that the tree had been removed by a fellow cyclist. She was now free to progress down the trail that brought her such joy. When we apologize for hurts we have caused others, it is as if we remove the obstacles in their paths. While advancement from pain is possible, this isn't generally a quick fix, because people can be very stubborn. Often they don't have just one tree blocking their way, but many.

I worked with an individual who made almost every decision for business a laborious battle. We often didn't see things eye-to-eye, from the short-term goals to the long-term, and this made every move toward progress a great difficulty. We had different visions and different ways to achieve them, which made even our successes muted, with many wounds and scars collected along the decision-making process. While many looking at this business didn't realize things were that difficult, I certainly did, and usually I found myself giving in to this individual so that there could be peace. What I wanted was a simple apology, or even an attempt on his part to understand my position, and while that would have made things easier for me, this individual saw no need to appease my frustrations. Maybe your spouse has said some horribly painful things to you, and you stew and wait for a hint of comprehension on her part that her words have hurt. What if she never gives you that apologetic word? We must have a way to move forward when other people use their power not to build but instead to destroy.

One of the ways we can advance toward freedom and beyond the emotional captivity of our past is to become agents of healing for others. With our insecurities and struggles, we can also administer healing, in both our words and our actions. As agents of healing, we have to be sensitive to others' receptivity to our words; without that receptivity, people may hold grudges against us and even actively work against our progress. It never hurts to be generous with our words, especially knowing how much healing can accompany them. We know that they are important because hurtful comments from others are often what keep our familiar grudges in place. We also need to be people of action. Righting wrongs is very difficult, but the effort of restitution can show our integrity and bring about healing.

We cannot say we are agents of healing if we are unwilling to do what it takes to bring about that healing. Have you ever noticed that what brings us together is usually not our charmed life and numerous successes? When we go through difficult times, often a person comes into our lives who really knows what we are going through. I remember traveling with the band and we had recently hired a new guitar player. He was to be my roommate as we traveled, probably because I sometimes had difficulty getting along with the other individual I worked with. This new member of the group had only been with us for a few weeks when something amazing happened as we talked one evening in our hotel room. He actually understood my feelings and frustrations. It was the strangest thing to be able to share something I was feeling and for him to articulate why I was struggling with that emotion. I was blown away! He was a lot younger than I, but as he shared some insights with me, I realized I wasn't crazy for feeling so frustrated and hurt. You and I are called to be that listening ear for those we encounter. We have a lot of experience feeling hurt by another's words and deeds, and it is this wounded part of ourselves that we can share with those who struggle beside us. Sometimes we just need someone to listen, and in our various relationships we can be that person.

When we realize the power we have to build up another with our words and deeds, life can become far more exciting as we put this ability into practice. We will be empowered and truly satisfied when we recognize that we are not in competition with others so much as members of one body collaborating for the betterment of one another. This longing to enhance another can be seen in many social justice programs, which emphasize the beauty in children and the need for their betterment, which often gets neglected. When we recognize that we have real power to help others succeed, achieve dreams, and make something of themselves, it can make all the difference in how we live our lives. Being a healer for others doesn't mean that we ourselves are entirely whole, but in some miraculous way, the focus upon another's betterment is a balm that soothes many of the wounds of our own lives.

THE SOLUTION: IT'S OK

While we strive to be agents of healing for others, and rejoice when another offers a much-needed apology, our inner need can and will be met in Christ, who willingly is our healer. Again, for many who have been hurt by the Church or by those claiming to follow Christ, this idea of Jesus as our Good Samaritan is very clouded. However, Jesus' tenacity in extending new opportunities in which we can see his sacred heart beating for us is a wonder to behold. And while the judgmental tendency of many Christians is disconcerting and hurtful in its recklessness, the acceptance of Jesus as the embodiment of love is the only way our need for love, acceptance, and healing can be met. I know this is an audacious claim, and yet I willingly stand by it: We need Jesus. The key that unlocks healing for our brokenness will be found in Jesus, but brokenness is not the only hinderance we face in trying to be people of purpose. At some point along the journey of life we realize that while people's actions toward us can be paralyzing, we ourselves have such a tendency toward weakness that we all seem to limp on this path of life right from the start! The weight of our own frailty can be another area of our lives that we often choose to ignore, but just as Jesus longs to be the true agent of healing for our wounded lives, he also wishes to be our strength when we run up against our weakness.

Remember our first couple, Adam and Eve, and their choice to ignore the Word of the Father? Because of their selfishness in denying the goodness of God, others were harmed rather than healed. Original sin results in a lack of grace, which is manifested in our hurtful and harmful actions. In order to be agents of healing and use our words to build rather than destroy, we must allow Jesus our Savior to take our wounds and wants and breathe new life into us. We need to let Jesus tear down our walls, because he will protect and provide for us, and we must take off our masks because he will truly love us as we are. We can allow Jesus into our lives or bury our pain in things that will never allow us to move beyond the impact of forbidden fruit. We are called to healing and invited to mediate healing to others, but we must say yes to Jesus, who is ready to listen and understand where we are in order to lead us to where we can be.

QUESTIONS

1. Can you talk about the various walls you have in your life? What led you to construct them?

2. Can you imagine a life without those walls? What would need to happen for them to come down?

3. What masks do you regularly wear? Why?

4. Can you remember a time someone actually saw the real you? Was this consoling or frightening?

5. What do you do when faced with a struggle or problem? Do you find yourself suppressing your feelings rather than dealing with them?

6. What needs to happen for you to experience healing?

7. Is it possible for you to be an agent of healing for others, even though you are not OK? Does this make you feel better?

FURTHER READING

1. *The Return of the Prodigal Son,* by Henri Nouwen

2. *Spirituality You Can Live With,* by Chris Padgett

CHAPTER 5:
THE WEIGHT

WE ARE ALL WEAK

About ten years ago I had open heart surgery. If you were wondering, no, I didn't die during the procedure. I am part pig now (which explains some of my weight and snoring issues, I suppose). I was born with a defective aortic valve. Over time, it eventually just wore out, as we all knew would happen. I couldn't do anything to change the fact that I was born with this partially closed valve. Inevitably it would just need to be replaced. Having the surgery was a very sobering moment in my family's journey. During the procedure and recovery I was entirely dependent upon others' medical expertise in order to live. My wife and I were very frightened and worried about the surgery, yet our faith held us together. I had been talking about Christ publicly for many years; it was time to really trust that he would be there for me as I potentially entered eternity. Thankfully I have been given many years to enjoy my family since that day, but in fact, my heart is still weak and that valve will eventually have to be replaced again.

Unless you have had a serious medical procedure, I am not sure you can understand the terror of having to go back and experience once again something that unnerved you. Waking up after the surgery, I felt so dehydrated. There was a large tube down my throat and it seemed I was barely able to inhale, let alone swallow. I desperately needed water, and had the primal urge to rip the tube from my throat so I could yell for just a drop. The only thing that kept me from doing this was a friend's advice before going into surgery. He is a nurse anesthetist and so he has some knowledge of pre- and postsurgical procedures. My friend warned me that waking up in ICU I would panic with the tube in my throat, but that I had to keep calm because taking it out would just delay its eventual removal, since they would have to put it back in again anyway. As his words echoed in my blurry consciousness it took every ounce of willpower not to panic.

I don't want to have to go through that again, but my heart is weak; I have very little say in the matter. My wife says that she feels the same panic when she thinks about having to have another C-section. The interesting thing for me was not just the impact of my physical weakness but also the emotional weakness I struggled with during recovery. I wondered if I would ever feel normal again. Would I ever get better? I couldn't see the future possibilities because I was so drained emotionally. Hope came in small moments of progress and affirming words from family and the nursing staff.

As a public speaker I often know when I am connecting with my audience. I believe that the Lord has given me a gift to somehow discern what story to tell in order to break through walls of skepticism, disinterest, and doubt. It is such a grace to flow with the rhythm of a crowd and bring them closer to the love of Christ. Often I will receive a lot of affirming words from those who attend the event, and the host is greatly pleased with my presentation, so much so that much of what I do is repeat business. However, there are occasions when I get a comment from someone that basically says I am completely ineffective at what I do. I can have a couple thousand people happy as a clam with what I say, but the one person in the audience who has a beef with me or my message preoccupies my mind. I mull over the words that person said or e-mailed, trying to formulate a perfect defense for someone who will not be convinced. It hurts, and I get frustrated that one person can impact my thinking so deeply. Thank God my wife is the exact opposite. The Lord knew I needed someone who can speak clearly to my wounded heart, lifting me out of the pit of second-guessing. I am weak, but he is giving me the strength to battle the wounds others have caused.

Acknowledging our weaknesses is difficult and we tend to avoid it at all costs. We have spent much of our lives trying to hide from our wounds. We also do our best to hide the weak areas of our character from others on a regular basis. The reasons why we desire to keep our weaknesses from the public eye are myriad, but suffice it to say we would rather be given the benefit of the doubt, have opportunities instead of being denied them, and keep potential "ammunition" from those who would willingly exploit our weakness for their benefit. The sobering clarity of our finite lives, emphasized by our varying weaknesses, seems to keep many people from stepping out and being fully who they are in Christ and for their families, but there is hope for all of us nonetheless.

Have you ever seen a baseball player as he swings the bat while he waits on deck? There are weights on the end of the bat that require the ballplayer to put more effort and energy into the swing. After the player has done a few practice swings, the weights come off and the bat feels exceptionally light. The power of the swing is enhanced because he has removed the excess weight from the bat. Physically we are limited; about that there is no dispute. I can say I would like to be an NBA player all I want, but my pear-shaped body seems more inclined toward wobbling than toward running, and gravity and I are fast friends—my vertical jump is probably, at best, a good two inches. I'm short, I was born with a heart condition, and come to find out, the vision in one of my eyes is worse than in the other. In other words, I won't be getting a call from the Miami Heat anytime soon . . . or ever! Some people have natural physical abilities that with training and practice can be refined and honed into excellence. Others have never even thought about a sport or activity, but from a friend's encouragement they try something and find that they are amazing at it.

We have intellectual limitations as well. I must have taken algebra at least—well, I was going to give you a number, but it would likely be wrong because I am absolutely horrible at math! I just couldn't understand why we had to put numbers and letters together in a math equation, and truth be told, I have never wanted to find y or x as an adult. Once when my daughter asked me if I could help her with her math problem, I looked her square (no pun intended this time) in the eye and said: No. She proceeded to read me the math problem—which, by the way, is the very thing that makes me dislike math—as she continued talking about a hypotenuse. I told her I had seen a hypotenuse at the zoo, but saw no reason to try and figure out a math equation involving this obese water creature, and what was she talking about anyway?

Weakness in this chapter is not primarily about a physical limitation or inability, although they are often catalysts for emotional struggles; rather, it is more about the emotional and psychological weight that keeps us from our true potential. While we have legitimate physical and intellectual limitations, the reality is we are all limitless in our spiritual potential. Our physical limitations can bleed over into our emotional outlook, but the grace provided to us is limitless, thereby offering spiritual heights previously unimagined. Spiritual weakness looks different for each person. Our walk and journey is unique. You could be a physically fit individual but very weak spiritually, or you could be truly handicapped physically but a spiritual giant.

The *Catechism of the Catholic Church* says that we are all religious beings (CCC 26, 27). Just look at all the religions in the world; the fact that there are so many says something about our desire for meaning amid the madness. When a person recognizes that he is not only flesh and blood, things change in how he lives his life. Within the Christian milieu we are invited to see that aligning ourselves with Jesus Christ can bring about a heroic way of living. We call these people saints, and if we look closely, we realize that they are all wounded and weak as well. In spite of—or maybe because of—the weaknesses and even the wounds of their past, they invite Christ into these areas and become great. What will your life look like if you let Christ into your weaknesses?

Keep this in mind: Grace builds on nature. In other words, God isn't disinterested in your human condition, with its weaknesses and handicaps; rather, he will not limit your ability to live heroically because of your physical or even emotional frailty, in that he gives you grace that manifests greatness in what many would see as an impossibility. The world waits with expectation and hope, wanting to know if we can move beyond our physical and emotional weaknesses. There is a problem, though, with reaching the limitless potential of our spiritual life, and it often comes down to a simple truth: We are free to believe in the victory offered us or not. We are free to remain weak or we can become strong. Remember, love must necessarily have the freedom to respond either in favor of or against someone in order to be authentic.

ADDRESSING THE PROBLEM

Let's address the problem head-on. It is OK to be weak. I am not sure why we have embraced the idea that we always have to be strong and always have to be knowledgeable and prepared for every scenario we face, but not only is it unrealistic; it is also unhealthy. I teach at a university, and I can tell you that if I ever feel like I've stopped learning because I have arrived intellectually, all of my students will be in trouble. I am asked questions that I don't know the answers to, and as a result I go and search them out. I've been speaking around the world for close to two decades, and there are still moments when I encounter a situation that is a little out of my comfort zone.

An intellectual weakness is one thing, but a greater example would be struggles with depression or marital conflict. What do we do with those weaknesses? Because my parents divorced and my father wasn't home to be an example, I have struggled on a daily basis with what it looks like to be a good father. Because of the marital struggle my parents went through, I don't have examples of how to work through difficulties faced in marriage, which makes me feel weak. A moment in which we realize our weakness can be a stepping stone to something dynamic, but it takes being fearless when it comes to that weakness. The problem of weakness is real for every person, but it is not the end of the story—or at least it should not be.

My wife, Linda, says I have thin skin. I feel things too deeply and take comments very personally. She says I'm a "sensie." (I try not to feel bad about that!) It came as a great surprise to me over the years that there were folks who actually didn't care for me. Linda may struggle with the opposite quality when it comes to people's comments and opinions. We could call her "lizard skin," but I imagine that would initiate an argument. I have often felt Linda's quick ability to move beyond others' opinions and comments would be so beneficial to have, but then that would upset the balance in our relationship. She needs someone with a sensitive heart and I need someone who's a bit tougher. These weak qualities—and both in their extreme applications are definite weaknesses—can be complemented by our being courageous together.

While many things we encounter can be stepping stones to a new moment of victory, there are a few things in life that can stop us cold. Death and abuse are obvious examples, and often we need the assistance of others to face these hurdles. We may be too weak to see the distance we have gone thus far, or unable to perceive the finish line through the inclement weather, and these places in our journey can be very dark and frightening. Weakness primarily originates from our actions or lack thereof. Will we accept the challenge before us or not? Will we ask for the aid of our neighbor or not? Will we allow someone to carry the heavy burden with us, or will we try and muscle through until we collapse in exhaustion?

Interestingly enough, Jesus himself allowed his physical weakness to become a reality. How so? The Incarnation allows for physical weakness! The omnipotent and omnipresent second person of the Trinity becomes specifically located in time as a baby. Babies are the embodiment of physical weakness. Infants can't feed, change, or care for themselves and are entirely dependent upon caregivers. They have little fingers that will one day grab the chocolate pudding on their own and break everything valuable in our homes, but it will take a long time for them to understand and put into practice their potential. Young children have muscles and arms that are unable to carry large objects, but as they grow they begin to realize what they are able to do. Jesus was entirely dependent upon Mary and Joseph, and while he had little fingers, it wouldn't be until he was older that he would take bread in his hands and institute the Eucharist for each of us. While he had muscles and arms as a child, he wouldn't be able to carry the cross until he was an adult. But even as an adult Jesus shows his weakness as he stumbles toward Calvary. Three times he falls under the weight of that cross, and in the end he is aided by Simon the Cyrene. Remember, God chose to become flesh and dwell among us. He chose to be fully human while being fully divine, and thus he chose to love within the limitations of time and space. Our Lord chose to be vulnerable so we could see what love looks like.

It is OK to be weak; it is part of our humanity. In addition to physical weakness, we often struggle with spiritual weakness. This is also OK, yet our Lord wants to take us to a deeper place, the place of his strength. We will always have the opportunity to remain stagnant, ineffective, and unproductive, but it certainly isn't the ideal. I believe it could also be said that the closer we move toward Christ the brighter the light will shine in our lives, revealing many areas of spiritual weakness that we were previously unaware of. When we rest in the reality of where we are spiritually, we can see more clearly where the Lord wants to take us. When we allow the Lord to extend to us his strength, we can find victory in personal battles that seemed insurmountable before. Whether it is a physical or a spiritual weakness, the opportunity for sanctity awaits the hungry heart.

OUR RESPONSE

How do we respond to this idea of accepting weakness as part of our humanity? We are free to respond in any way that we wish. We can either pretend we are not weak or we can give up the pretense and acknowledge that we are not as strong as we have led others to believe.

Pretend we are not weak

Pretending we are not weak is a lot easier than acknowledging our deficiencies, but it isn't the path leading to strength. Exaggeration may fool others, but in the end we have not fooled ourselves. Have you ever met a drug addict or an alcoholic? If people who struggle with addiction can admit they have a problem, they can journey toward a new way of living. That vulnerability is the first step, and it can be terribly difficult to acknowledge. When people under the guise of ignorance come to the end of trying to battle what they cannot destroy, they paradoxically find themselves with the power to do what they were previously unable to accomplish. Weakness points out the need; once this happens, the need can be met. We must give up trying to invent new ways of being masters of disguise and simply realize our humanity. Everyone has desire, and this can be either ordered or disordered. How we respond to those desires will enable us to be either successful or self-destructive.

Let's use a different example. A person who is addicted to gambling has a disordered desire. How she responds to that desire will enable her to either be victorious over this area of weakness or give in to it. If a person establishes a new road, acknowledging the path she was on as destructive and one that sapped her of strength, she can find a new outcome and a different destination. It always comes down to seeing her weakness and making her choices fall in step with the plan that enables success. We have to give up on the old way and try the new path, ridding ourselves of the weight that's holding us down.

Give up

Giving up on the familiar path we are so used to is not easy, but it is the path to victory. There is a very popular book from the 1990s called *Who Moved My Cheese?* The main point of the book is based on the idea of individuals moving on with change instead of stewing over the things in their lives that have not remained the same. It invites people to find new pathways and opportunities instead of being angry that things have moved or changed. While many of us keep looking for the rush, the high, or the meaning found in the familiar path, acknowledging that it has led us to defeat leaves only one real solution: Get on a new path! We have to stop lugging around the weight of false ideas and understandings of ourselves, and embrace the potential of a life without that weight.

Giving up on the old habits and familiar ways is not possible unless we acknowledge we are weak and heavy laden. True success can be found in Christ, who is the way! His invitation to come to him even if we are weak and heavy laden still extends to you and me, but we must be willing to give up on the old path and the familiarity of the weight that we carry, and believe that there is a solution.

THE SOLUTION: IT'S OK

The solution is simple: With the love Jesus offers you, it is going to be OK. You have the choice to lean upon Christ Jesus, who will be your Simon of Cyrene. Christ will be your strength. This is not an empty promise—a true strength is given to endure the storms we face. Remember, Jesus wants you to be healthy and whole even more than you do, and so he offers you exactly what you need to obtain satisfaction.

GRACE: PRAYER/SACRAMENTS

Jesus knows that we all were born with spiritually weak hearts because of sin. He is the master surgeon; he knows we can't fix ourselves and that we need to rely on his expertise to replace and heal our original wounds. No matter how many times we stumble on our weakness, he will always be there to give us strength and courage.

The need for Jesus will always be there; we just have to realize it so we can depend fully on him. It really will be OK when you let Jesus love you right where you are. He is not afraid of your weakness. He knows you struggle with your marriage, and he knows you lose your temper with your children. Jesus understands that you want more for your life than just going through the motions, and so he comes to you ready to be your hero.

We often think that we will inconvenience God if we ask for forgiveness once again for a familiar sin, or that we have worn out our welcome because we are weak, but the opposite is true. Jesus longs to forgive us and desires to be with us amid all our human frailty. The proof of his love for humanity is in his Incarnation, death, burial, and Resurrection. The love God has for us is what we most need to recognize in order to confidently offer him our weakness. This is a new path for us, but it is offered nonetheless. Will you walk with Jesus toward healing?

When I was young my grandmother had the "Footprints" poem hung up in the bathroom. I am not sure when I first noticed it, but I can recall reading it for the first time as a young boy. I was very touched, even moved a bit emotionally. If you haven't read it, I would suggest you give it a quick glance. The story is simple: There are two sets of footprints in the sand, representing an individual and the Lord, but during the individual's greatest struggles in life only one set of prints is visible. The person asks the Lord why he abandoned him during the great crises he faced, and the Lord's response beautifully reveals that there is only one set of footprints because he was carrying the wounded traveler. This is exactly what I want you to realize and believe. Jesus is OK if you are physically and spiritually weak, because his arms are strong enough to carry you. You are weak but he is strong. I hope you are beginning to see that you are loved far more than you have ever imagined.

QUESTIONS

1. In what way do you feel physically weak?

2. Has your physical weakness impacted your emotions? How?

3. Can you imagine being spiritually strong? What would need to happen for this to come about?

4. How do you deal with your emotional and spiritual weaknesses? Do you face them or ignore them?

5. Can you see that it is OK to be weak? How can Jesus love you in your weakness today?

FURTHER READING

1. *Who Moved My Cheese?* by Spencer Johnson

2. The book of Jonah

3. "Footprints in the Sand," by Mary Stevenson

CHAPTER 6:

THE WANT

When we do not find satisfaction for our needs in Christ we will eventually try and fill the chasm with various wants. Because wants are unable to fill the growing emptiness, we become more broken over time and inevitably more weak. The culmination of the two, along with despair, is what I mean by this next point, facing our emptiness.

Emptiness has an impact upon our lives, whether we experience it ourselves or know others who find themselves lost within its depths. When this recognition of emptiness happens, there is little that can be said to convince someone to simply move beyond it. We might look at the individual and conclude that if he would only try again he may succeed and pull himself out of his rut. While that might work for some individuals who are trying to cope with their brokenness, emptiness is a state in which the person has no will to see what a future can look like. The overwhelming want eventually becomes singular as despair leads to a desire for death. I have met some people in this lonely place, and it can be haunting. The realization that they are on the brink of some final decisions fills the onlooker with desperation. A mother who has lost a child, a father who is no longer able to take care of his family, or a teen who can't deal with the pain anymore all know emptiness too well. Their eyes are vacant and their strength is gone; they are truly empty.

So what about you? If you are found wrecked and lost in this emptiness, it is likely that you won't see others who may be struggling with the same thing. It is probable that for you everything is so dark that the idea of helping another seems like hypocrisy. You have nothing to give, and you feel unable to fix even yourself, since you are unable to articulate what it is you need. Maybe you struggle with anger issues. Every time you ask your children to clean up, do homework, or be quiet, they do the opposite. It seems that the smallest thing can set you off. Constant overreaction has created a habit that frightens you. This is not what you wanted, and it seems impossible to change. As you brush up against this emptiness, you react even more in anger, unable to stop what you know is wrong. Possibly you have struggled with an addiction to pornography, drugs, or alcohol. Every time you try and start over it seems all efforts are for naught as you fall once again to the familiar vice. You can't see a way out of this hole, and conclude that giving up may be the only thing you can commit to. Maybe it started with a struggle with being overweight. Over time you have found that everything you try to counter this vice simply fails. You begin to feel such despair, and your entire being is hopelessly caught in self-loathing. The words people have uttered toward you sink deep, and the looks pierce your heart, affirming your fear that you are unlovable, unworthy of God's love, and unable to be someone different. The enemy thrives in this self-deprecation. For you, maybe the longing for hope is gone.

I would like to emphasize that God's love for you is not based upon your weight. While you strive and fail to control overeating, you must hear this word of truth, which may be difficult to believe: You matter. The love God has for you is unprecedented. There will never be another individual like you, and while you may struggle with overeating, it is no worse than another's struggle with lust. We all battle passions that are disordered, but Jesus will give us the victory even if we can't believe this fact. Hold tightly to the words of Christ in which he calls for those who are weak and heavy laden, because it is to you that he will give rest. Take courage in the fact that while others have passed by your wounds and failings, Jesus not only stops for you but he also cares for the needs in your life. Believe that even in your darkest hour Jesus is there, because he truly does love you.

IS THERE HOPE?

Is there hope for an individual in this dark place? This is a very important question. The answer is simply yes. When I was younger my grandmother, who was blind and inclined to feed me healthy cereal, would have me read to her the grocery coupons that came in the paper. She would ask me to tell her what the product was and what sale was being offered. The description and specifics given were necessary. I would hand them to her when we finished, and while it was time consuming, she truly couldn't have done this on her own. What is being offered to people who are empty is something they cannot see on their own. We have to take time—and it will take a lot more than most people are willing to invest in others—to remind them that they are not alone, that there is hope. In fact, I often think people just want to offer a quick cliché to those who struggle, expecting that people should just snap out of their funk, probably because they are afraid of the emptiness they behold in others. After all, if we just gave them such relevant advice, then haven't we done our part? The time it will take for people to journey out of emptiness is varied, but one thing it is not is quick. Describing what their world can look like is almost like an artist painting a picture right before another's eyes. It will take time, and many of the images will not make sense right away, but in the end there will be a perspective given that can take the viewer to someplace new.

THE PROBLEM

The problem we have to address when dealing with emptiness is not that there is no way toward fulfillment, but that most people are not willing to take the time to invest in another person for as long as it takes to show signs of improvement. When I was in Boston and the mother of an addict came up to me, I could see the sorrow and brokenness in her eyes. She was exhausted and frustrated, weak and at her wits' end. She wanted desperately for her daughter to be whole, but the truth of the situation she faced was dire. Her daughter had been kicked out of rehab again and they were waiting for an opening in another facility. She looked at me and said that when she got home that evening she would just tell her daughter that she loved her, just the way she was. As a result of her daughter's emptiness, the mother has to face her own emptiness, which is her parental inability to alleviate or control her child's pain.

The willingness to be with people and love them as they are may be painful, because we might find ourselves having to address the deep insecurities and ache that we have hidden for so long. The individual who is lost in emptiness inevitably will be healed when loved by another who recognizes such dizzying pain, and the two can assist one another. This must be our response to people enveloped in emptiness. When we begin to really care for others, we will do whatever it takes for as long as it takes to assist them as Christ has helped us over time. The things that we say to people really are of great import, but our presence says clearly what our words fail to: that they are worthy and valuable to us just the way they are.

For those of you who are so empty right now, it may seem that there isn't anyone who will walk with you in this dark time. If that lack of companionship is your reality, then I would strongly urge you to go to the Blessed Sacrament once a day for a brief period of time and ask that Jesus be that friend who walks with you toward the light. This is not a cliché! The best I can do as a friend for those who struggle with emptiness is to imitate Jesus' love and point them to him. If you, feeling alone, run directly to Jesus, I guarantee that he will not give up on you. Even if you sit and stare at the Eucharist, saying nothing, Jesus sees your broken heart and that deep emptiness. He will pour love into your life even if you can't feel anything. Run to Jesus' love, because he will always fill your heart.

OUR RESPONSE

So what will our response be to those we love who have experienced emptiness? How will we address our own encounters with such emptiness? We will either buckle up and realize that a long journey awaits us, or we will be given over to despair. This moment is critical. If it is a friend or family member, we are likely to go a greater distance with him or her in trying to find the path out of emptiness, but even here the growing urge to give up is regularly felt. Feelings of hopelessness grow with each failed attempt. I have a friend who shared the story of his brother, who was a drug addict. There was nothing pretty about that journey. The moment when he walked in and saw his father holding his brother down, waiting for the police to arrive, is one that would bring most families to the point of hopelessness and surrender. A girl I met in Connecticut told me how she walked upstairs and saw her sobbing father holding her dead brother.

When we notice people's emptiness we may feel the urge to flee. It is as if fear is driving us from such a horrific place; our primal instincts are trying to protect us from such hopelessness. We will likely be present with them as they repeatedly try and articulate their emptiness, or we will give in to despair ourselves, concluding that there is no road out of that hell, or that they are a lost cause. While these examples are not normal for most of us, we do feel this desperation and hopeless emptiness when tragedy befalls our country or cities. As we all watch the horror of the numerous school shootings, we touch emptiness, and as we remember the attacks on 9/11, we are reminded that so much is out of our control. The actions of others impacting us negatively can be a stepping stone to emptiness. So what is our hope? What is the solution for us in the realm of so much that we cannot control?

THE SOLUTION: IT'S OK

We must hold on to the promise that even in the chaos and horrible difficulties of life it's going to be OK, but only in Christ. I am not dismissing the fact that there is a struggle, nor am I saying that such horrific events are OK. But amid the great external or internal conflict, there is a solution that is beyond even the agony of struggling out of despair. Jesus Christ finds a way to be present in our greatest emptiness. I certainly don't know how he does this, but I can only conclude that it has to do with his unconditional love for even the most wounded. Consider the one sheep that wanders off, and know that Jesus will go after that sheep so that it can be reunited with its community. Jesus is not afraid of our emptiness; he will be the only one who can truly fill us to the point of moving forward.

Recently a woman told me about the death of her son a few years ago. He'd had a life of constant suffering, and in her grieving she felt every emotion. In my talk that night I had spoken about the virtue of justice, how it is giving to God what he is due, and giving to man what he is due. She found such consolation in realizing that her son's death was not the end of something, but the beginning of time with Christ, which was the justice he was due for all the suffering he had experienced. I think she found a bit of consolation in knowing that her suffering and moments of despair were not in vain. In addition to this woman, one of the leaders of the event came up to me during the prayer service, along with her son and daughter. They asked me to pray for them because her husband had died a few months ago. I looked at her and simply said that there was nothing I could offer that would make it better, except the fact that Jesus was truly with them.

Even the people who appear to have it all together are struggling with deep pain and a great want. The pain people are processing in this world can be overwhelming. Just because you are in a leadership position does not mean that you don't feel empty; this ache and want is something we all have to face in varying degrees. So realize that this is a long journey out of emptiness for you and others, brought about by seeing things from a different perspective. God is providing a new beginning for you through the agents of healing he brings your way, but you also have a chance to share your journey with others who are experiencing the despair and emptiness that you have known so well. It is OK to be empty, because Christ will find us and paint a path back to health.

One of the beautiful teachings of the Catholic Church is redemptive suffering. When we place our pain and sorrow, our brokenness and weakness and even emptiness into the passion of Christ, something miraculous happens. The pain doesn't necessarily go away, but placing it upon the cross with Jesus and allowing him to offer it to the Father in the love of the Spirit makes our great loss a great gain in the spiritual journey of another. The more we do this, the greater our hearts will grow in their capacity to love not only ourselves but also the many others who are crippled with emptiness. Jesus gives us a place to put our pain so that we can move from that darkness into his light. We are invited to an abundant life, even if we have to travel great distances to see this.

CHRIST WILL FILL US TO OVERFLOWING

I want to explain what I mean by a life "filled to overflowing," because this could be misunderstood. I am not saying we will always be happy, that our past will somehow not be messy, or that we will never be broken and struggle with weakness or emptiness. If that is the case, then how can we hope to be filled to overflowing with Christ, which is what we are promised in the Scriptures? Jesus uses an analogy of a wineskin: We are invited to have new wine placed within new wineskins, because putting new wine into an old wineskin would cause it to rupture. The wine in the new container is not limitless; the skin must always be refilled. In other words, we need a constant intake of new wine because it will be depleted over time. If a person goes through life and doesn't allow the wineskin to be renewed, or doesn't fill it with the grace of God as the wine is depleted, the result will be an empty wineskin. We must always stay near the source that fills our wineskin. We also need new wineskins to replace our battered ones. I believe that accepting Christ's love for us in our deep pain is the new wineskin, and while we can remember the ache and loss, the pain and struggle we have and experience, the new skin will not rupture, because what Jesus fills us with is exactly what we need.

The world tries to fill our emptiness with an old wine in our old skins, and this causes deep cracks over time. The old wine is promises broken and pain given in relationships without healing. It is the world insisting we follow a wide path. The old wine is all of the artificial things we put into our lives that are supposed to help us find fulfillment but instead leave us empty or rotting within. Chemical dependency, careless or bad relationships, and entertaining ourselves to death are all ways that we try and fill ourselves, but we can't handle that toxic intake without breaking down. Christ is the one with the never-ending supply of new wine—not us, and not the world. We need to place ourselves under the faucet of his love, and begin to let the healing and filling of mercy and acceptance take place.

In light of this, here is the one great benefit of being empty: When people are truly empty of all hope and understanding of a way out of the mess, and when they have nothing left of themselves to make the journey back to healing and strength, the only way they will be filled is by another pouring into them what will fill and heal them. Who the source is and what goes into us will determine the outcome. Those in despair let the lies of the enemy be poured into them, and the result is death. For those who can glimpse a new picture from Christ's filling, there can be an abundance, which will overflow. Most of the time, people in a decent place with God want to be filled more with the love of Christ, but they struggle with trying to let go of selfishness and other "self" hindrances. They still want to be in control, still want to have things done their way, still want certain masks in place and certain rooms within them to remain off-limits to God. Empty individuals know they have no control and no agenda, because all previous attempts have failed. They can't wear a mask and there are no barriers or walls; they are simply vacated homes ready for demolition. The goodness of God can fill the empty person completely, which is the miraculous abundant life that we need. We won't be able to move forward until we allow Christ to fill us, and then we will need to learn how to let Christ continue to do so as we begin our new journeys.

So where are you in your spiritual journey? Are you feeling overwhelmed by your responsibilities, or stressed by your inability to make everything work and fall in step with your plans? Are you tired of trying to be better, knowing you'll just fail again? If so, it's OK. You are not horrible for feeling this way, and it isn't uncommon to want to give up struggling. Jesus comes to you and is willing to be with you for as long as it takes to bring you into an abundant life. He will never leave you or forsake you. Jesus is not tired of listening to your irritations and frustrations, and he willingly listens to all of your concerns. He knows your anger and is not deterred from you. Jesus sees your exhaustion and will not give up fighting on your behalf. You are not alone, and if you can just see that he is there, I know it will give you the perspective you need to say yes to another day. One of those days, maybe in the distant future, you will fully believe that he has loved you all along, and suddenly you will feel new wine pouring into you, healing you, and overflowing from you. Be encouraged—you are going to be OK. Most of us are not lost completely in despair. The weight of our concerns often feels manageable, even if those concerns are burdensome. If we don't allow Christ to refresh us, the exhaustion will lead to despair and our emptiness will rob us of any joy and hope. Those who find themselves on the edge or even lost must embrace the same truth as those who are not overwhelmed: Christ is in us. Jesus Christ wants to fill us with himself so that we can be the best us we can be. Jesus meets you right where you are and it's OK, because he knows exactly the healing you will need to be satisfied.

QUESTIONS

1. Do you know someone who is struggling with emptiness? How does this make you feel?

2. Have you ever felt like you were empty? How did the people around you make you feel?

3. Is it possible that you have been trying to satisfy yourself with the old wine of the world? In what ways are you trying to fill this emptiness?

4. Will you ask Jesus to fill you, even if you don't feel anything, so that you can begin to have a new perspective on suffering?

5. If you could offer all of your pain up for someone else to be better, who would that be?

FURTHER READING

1. *Can You Drink the Cup?* by Henri J. M. Nouwen

CHAPTER 7:

BE NEEDY: RECOGNIZING OUR NEED IS THE BEGINNING OF HEALING

We must be willing to acknowledge that we are needy in order to have an abundant life. Because we have spent a lot of time trying to keep our brokenness and weakness from others, the idea that our neediness will lead to abundance in our lives seems far-fetched. It is a paradox. Let's step back and look at a basic point that might easily be forgotten: We are intentional and singular, and in the words of the philosopher Dr. John Crosby, we are incommunicable. There will never be another individual who thinks about life the same way you do, nor will there be anyone who will articulate need in the same way. Even if you are a twin, triplet, etc., you are entirely unique. While it is our temptation to compare ourselves with our siblings or friends, the unique reality of each person is so important that comparison only dampens what we are called to be.

When I was a kid, my two best friends were identical twins. There were times they would slip into a different classroom and pretend to be the other brother without their teacher realizing this had happened. They were identical in appearance, and certainly had similar mannerisms and qualities. While they could fool many teachers and other classmates, they were unable to pull the wool over my eyes. Why? Because they were my best friends. I could tell the difference. We are known by God, and while that may be a simple declaration that many have heard before, it is important to reiterate the fact that God doesn't want us to be like someone else.

A wonderful quote by Saint Francis de Sales says, "Be who God made you to be, and be that perfectly well." What if we could truly be ourselves? What if we could rest and be accepted as we are? This is the true reality behind the Gospel message, which speaks of a God who knows us so well that each hair upon our heads is counted. Not a sparrow falls to the ground without his knowledge, and God created us in such a way that we long for this type of acceptance.

Unfortunately, we often find a lack of acceptance when we go to church. Maybe our clothing is perceived to be too casual, or our dress too short, or maybe we feel like every eye is turned upon us because we have a tattoo or nose piercing. It seems that so much of the Christianity that we encounter is people insisting we look and act like them. Often, instead of being loved as we are, we find a subtle—or not so subtle—pressure to be just like everyone else. So, unfortunately, the mask goes up, even in the place where we should be able to finally just be ourselves. Maybe the way to make this transition toward an authentic way of living is to simply be countercultural, even in our churches, if necessary.

Really, we are all people of great need. This need is why we go to church in the first place—because we recognize that there is a longing for community and a need for one who is greater than we are. When people find opposition and confrontation in this place of potential rest, often it results in many of them leaving the church. This exodus from the parish community is one that causes those departing to hold on to great bitterness. The hurt inflicted by fellow followers of Christ can be often more painful than anything we experience in our workplaces, and unless you've encountered this rejection, it is hard for you to sympathize with the disenfranchised. We all need Jesus, and he is not waiting for us to be like everyone else; instead, he wants us to embrace our uniqueness and let his love satisfy our need. This satisfying love of Jesus does not cause us to look like those around us, because God does not make duplicate saints. When we allow Jesus to come into our neediness, whether it is the constant need for affirmation, the feelings of insecurity and fear, the internal dialogue that we carry on with all our imaginary enemies, the ache from past humiliations, or an ambiguous sense of angst, our lives can find true rest with his presence. We need Jesus, but will we allow him to satisfy us?

God made us to be people of need, and he provided his Church as a safe haven for his followers to be refreshed and fed. When a parish is willing to love those who don't meet the standards of the world, we become effective and productive, because love is the enactment and pressing out of the cross. Being needy is an acceptance of our humanity. Being needy is a proclamation of our human condition. Being needy is exactly what Jesus has come to satisfy. When we refuse to face our neediness, we become judgmental of others. When we ignore our need, we often deflect from our flaws and point out those of our neighbors. It takes a lot of humility to actually face our neediness. Remember Adam and Eve in the Garden of Eden right after they fall from grace. As God comes and seeks Adam out, Adam blames Eve and Eve blames the serpent for their failing. They deflect from their own actions, hoping to lessen the consequences for themselves. We are never able to hide from what we have done and what we have failed to do. Our need cannot be filled by diverting to others our failed attempts at satisfying ourselves with a want.

When we enter a church and make the sign of the cross with the holy water, it is an acknowledgment that we were the recipients of the new life in baptism. The sign of the cross over ourselves is not a mindless act; rather, it is a bodily declaration that Jesus Christ has seen our need and offered us healing. When we say the words together, "Lord have mercy, Christ have mercy, Lord have mercy," we are acknowledging our need. No matter our socioeconomic status or our race, in Christ we all gather, acknowledging our need for his salvific work. Being willing to speak about our need for Christ to others outside of the Church is an act of heroic belief that unfortunately is difficult to do when we feel that those within the Church walls have no tolerance for our failings and weaknesses. I am sympathetic to this plight and I can honestly say that my family and I have experienced this type of hypocrisy.

Many years ago, my wife gathered our small children from the four corners of our home, and after much effort made her way to a local Catholic church to attend Mass. She was alone with the kids since I was off on a ministry trip. Having dressed the children, then buckled and unbuckled them from the car seats of our occasionally working vehicle, she lugged the baby and toddlers into the one place she knew she could find peace and acceptance: the house of God. Walking into the church with sweat pouring from her brow, she settled the kids into the pew, doing her best to keep the little ones quiet, all the while breathing a sigh of relief that at least one thing in her day was worthwhile, even if it was the equivalent of running a marathon. Getting to church was a priority amid the chaos of life, and she'd arrived before the distribution of Communion, so that was a miracle in and of itself! At the end of Mass an elderly gentleman—and I use the term *gentleman* loosely—leaned forward and said, "Could you stop bringing your distractions to church?" It took everything she had not to want to sever his head from his body. She left the church battered and bruised, uncared for and wounded. Why is it that so often the people who should love and care for us are the ones who actually hurt us the most?

Recently I stopped by a friend's house and he told me that he found it providential that I had pulled in at just that moment. He had been thinking of me and was planning on calling the house to vent about a few pressing issues. This friend of mine is covered in tattoos from head to toe, and while he looks a little rough on the outside, his heart is pure gold. For years he has been caring for and sharing his life and faith with all the inner-city kids in our town. In fact, every year, dozens of multinational, financially deprived, and wounded kids willingly choose to enter the Catholic Church because of his care and concern for their lives. He has seen it all! When an eleven-year-old girl announces that she is pregnant, or when a young man says that he felt God say he was going to do what the man with the gold thing was doing (a priest processing with the Eucharist in a monstrance), he considers his efforts to be exactly what Jesus had in mind when he told us to go into all of the world and preach the Good News. These kids share with him their family chaos, their dreams and hopes, and we get to have him as a member of our Church. My friend wanted to talk to me because the church staff announced to him that they had decided they wanted him to move his ministry off of church property, for many unfounded reasons. In the end, the concerns could have been easily countered or addressed, but he had to leave nonetheless. Why is it that the people who claim to really want to minister to the down-and-out actually want the kids to be down and away from their line of sight? It is this type of hypocrisy and insensitivity that has driven people away from the Church! If inner-city kids can't find in the Church an oasis and refuge from their problems, we are in a crisis.

If I recognize that the need for Jesus is a deep reality in me and in those around me, and I am willing to accept it instead of deflect from my failings, then I will be able to love those who deflect from their pain. I'll understand a bit more why they are acting in a manner that is minimizing who they can be. It won't make their actions right, but I will have a deeper understanding of how hurt they are. In order for me to have this perspective, I must come to Jesus for him to meet my need. Jesus is really giving himself to me in the Eucharist and the sacrament of reconciliation. My need for him is tangibly—not theoretically—met in the sacrament of sacraments. When I go to confession I am not imagining my need being met by Jesus; it in fact is actually met.

Yes, there are difficult people we will face in our families, work environments, and even in church, but we are not to compare ourselves with them, because Jesus is enabling us to be the saints he wants us to be, the saints who live life to the fullest even when they're misunderstood and judged. From the elderly man's comment about my kids being a distraction, to the parish deciding to evict the urban ministry from its grounds, to the rude behavior of a few parish members and insensitive comments from clergy, it all just makes a person feel that he is more accepted in a bar than in this house of worship.

But I don't stumble into church because people treat me with respect, even though they should. I don't enter my local parish because the pastor knows how to speak in an understanding way to me, although he should. I go to the church, with all of its flaws and mess, because I still need Jesus. I am still that broken and weak man I was, and while I've tried to drown a few of my sorrows in my fair share of drink, in the end it is only Jesus who can meet my need. The true presence of Jesus in the Eucharist is there for me, meeting my need, even when I am receiving the evil eye from an old lady in the opposite pew. (Either that or she needs a new prescription for her glasses!) Jesus is truly ready to give himself to me entirely, even if the homily was horrible. I go to church because I need Jesus to meet my need, and in fact he does. We may ask ourselves why Christ chooses to come to us through church and not through an afternoon relaxing on a sailboat. While God certainly calms our hearts as we walk about and enjoy his creative splendor, the sacraments give to us the fullness of Christ in very specific ways, which in fact meet a specific need that God knew could only be met in that way.

My wife likes to ride her bike religiously, and by "likes," I mean "obsessively loves in an addictive manner." This satisfies a basic need she has for quiet, nature, and exercise. But a bike ride will not meet the profound need we have for community and communion that Christ gives to us in the Eucharist. Think of it this way: You were made to be in communion with others and to have an encounter with God. This can happen in a variety of ways, but the ultimate way is by receiving Jesus in the Eucharist. Even when you are ignored by parishioners, you are not ignored by Jesus, who made it possible to have an intimate encounter with him. You can even be spoken against and hurt by people who should know better, but in order to satisfy the great need you have, Jesus gives himself to you in the Eucharist, which will satisfy you even if you don't feel him.

We were made to need fellowship, and God gives to us this true fellowship in the Eucharist. Being needy isn't a vice; rather, it is a catalyst that enables us to be finally satisfied and accepted. I sure wish this truth could resonate in the hearts of all those Catholics who have walked away from the Church, because while the reasons for leaving are understandable and often explainable, in the end the need remains unmet as they go from one thing to another in an attempt to find peace. If we can acknowledge that God accepts us in our neediness, and ignore the junk that seems to litter the lives of many of our religious friends, we can become an agent of healing as well as further our own efforts toward wholeness.

What every human person needs is a living relationship with Jesus. I know this sounds like a cliché to many outside the faith, but Jesus truly does accept us and offer us community and communion. "While you were yet sinners, I died for you." (Romans 5:8) Jesus isn't waiting for us to be better in order to love us. He sees our need and comes to us like the Good Samaritan. There is no hesitation from our Savior in extending to us that love we need. Christ waits for us to acknowledge our need for him. He will not force us to receive what he offers, so in the end the choice is ours: Do we want our need to be met? Christ wants to satisfy that need.

QUESTIONS

1. Why is it so difficult for us to acknowledge our need? How do you try and address your need?

2. Can you see that Jesus is willing to accept you amid your failings?

3. What will it look like if you let Jesus meet your need?

4. If Jesus is meeting your need, how will this free you to accept others who are trying to avoid facing their need?

FURTHER READING

1. *Adam: God's Beloved,* by Henri J. M. Nouwen

CHAPTER 8:

RISK IT: BE VULNERABLE

Within this book thus far we have talked about our brokenness, weaknesses, and emptiness and the fact that Christ is present for us in all of them. The pains and struggles are real, but we will be OK because of Jesus' tenacious love. If we will be vulnerable and open with the struggles we have gone through, in Christ, this honesty can help us to be agents of healing for those we encounter. When we risk our pride by sharing our journey of struggles, there are usually two possible results. The first is that we will be judged by others who think we are a horrible wreck. That's OK, but it can hurt to see that some people's love for us is so superficial. The other possibility of sharing or risking our vulnerability with others is that we will bring a confidence and hope to people that God will meet their needs as he has met ours. There is a balance in this vulnerability, of course, because we wouldn't disclose anything to someone that would be harmful or lead another to sin, but there are times in our lives when we can truly be open with others and help them journey closer to Jesus. When you find out about the struggles of someone who has been such a great leader and influence in your life, often you feel hope, because God working in them is proof positive that he will work in you.

Many years ago, I was traveling around with a band. You may have heard of us: Boyz II Men. OK, I wasn't in that band. I was in a contemporary Christian group called Scarecrow and Tinmen. On a very long tour, we were being housed at a retreat center and as was (and still is) my habit, I stumbled toward the bookshelves in order to satiate my addiction for spiritual writings. Scanning the titles, I found an author I had heard of but never really appreciated: Henri Nouwen. My only exposure to this priest's writings was when a "liberal" Protestant professor required us to read one of Nouwen's books on ministry. I was so unsettled at the time because as a Protestant I thought, What could a Catholic priest have to say about effective ministry? I am not sure which book of his I grabbed that afternoon, but I devoured it. I can't even describe the connection I had with his writing, except to say that I immediately felt a compulsion to read everything I could by this Catholic priest.

When I read his book *The Genesee Diary*, I think something profound happened in my understanding of what ministry and spirituality are supposed to be. While I had spent most of my life trying to crush every possible sin and unholy thought, hiding—at times even from myself—my pharisaical tendencies, Henri Nouwen wrote down all of his flaws for the world to read. He talked about wanting to be accepted, feeling insecure, and having struggles with the people he worked with. He articulated his wounded emotions masterfully, at times in a very raw fashion, not caring if people found him broken and weak. In fact, he regularly emphasized his wounded heart, because he honestly believed that this was the most authentic way for him to heal others and in turn be healed himself. It was a mind-blowing approach to spirituality for me. Why would you tell others how messed up you are? Why wouldn't you hold back from the public eye all those insecurities? I mean, sure, you can occasionally allude to a struggle, or make vague references to the old days when you were not following Christ, but Nouwen would talk about how hurt he was right there in the moment he was writing. It was like we were invited into his journal entries! Instead of being put off by this messy man, I found myself growing in hope. If this spiritual leader could be so open about his struggles and was striving to find Christ in his pain, then so could I. He would insist that if we could let Christ heal us of those wounds, then we could be free to love people and heal them in their wounded state of being. Henri Nouwen truly changed my life.

The person who finds her need being met in Christ has a decision to make. Will she be a person of healing for others or will she become one of the many "well-fed" Christians who keep what they have for themselves? Let's reflect upon the parable of the talents (Matthew 25:4–30). Each individual was given a certain amount of talents in which he could invest. When the time of accounting arrived, all showed what they had gained with the initial investment. Remember the one who was afraid to invest his talent (verse 25)? He was reproved, not because he failed in his investment, but because he didn't invest in anything at all. God gives to us gifts and talents, which are meant to bring peace and growth for us and others. The person who becomes an agent of healing for others is the one who finds himself met by Christ, and moving forward in gratitude he desires to bless others. The person who becomes a spiritual glutton is afraid of failing or being judged and so he ends up being ineffective in touching the lives of those around him.

Let's look at the spiritual glutton. When we finally come down to the basic reality of Christianity, it is not about knowledge; rather, it is about a relationship. The information we receive can help us trust and live for Christ more, but Jesus is not someone we need to simply learn about so that we can sound spiritual or fix everybody else's spiritual deficiencies. We don't want to just *sound* spiritual; we must *be* spiritual. Spirituality, though, is not some ethereal, non-corporeal state of being. Being truly spiritual means that we meet the needs of the body of Christ. This is why a person in leadership in a church can't simply say to someone, "Be warm and be filled," without actually meeting the needs of the person by giving her food and drink (cf. James 2:16). True religion impacts people around us and makes them better. The spiritual glutton is simply hoarding his gifts and talents, which, with his needs met, unfortunately remain idle. This is a toxic place, because if you don't give what you've been given, you will find that rot sets in. This is why many people become pharisaical. In the Old Testament the children of Israel were in the dessert for more than forty years. Whenever they tried to hoard the manna that was provided for their daily sustenance, it would rot (Exodus 16:20). God wanted them to depend upon him daily. They would consume what they were given and it would enable them to move forward, hopefully in obedience, into the Promised Land. Unfortunately, they bickered, fought, complained, and became content in the desert. They lost their vision of the Promised Land and as a result became sinful. We are all called to take our "daily bread," and hopefully that heavenly meal will enable us to enter the Promised Land. We can depend upon God's provision, which he has abundantly given us with the "bread from heaven," or we can be like the Israelites and wander around aimlessly, complaining and grumbling.

The individual who allows Christ to meet her needs on a daily basis remembers that she will never be in a place independent of his provision. The constant need being met by Jesus removes the sin of pride. We are unable to satisfy our hunger, but in Christ we are truly provided for and nourished. So what do we do with this provision and nourishment? We aid others in coming to Christ. The strength we find in Jesus is given so that we can point others to the well that quenches our thirst. We will certainly find ourselves exhausted and drained as we share our lives and wounded hearts with others, but recognizing that we don't need their affirmation or consolation in order to be healed enables us to be present for others. We have a ministry of presence because of Jesus' true gift of self to us. This is a truth that can change lives! It certainly has changed mine.

I often feel that we live what we believe to be true. So often, we nod our heads in agreement at spiritual insights, and then with our lives we move and act based on opposite beliefs. For example, I think most of us would acknowledge that Jesus is our Savior and wants to provide for us and care for us in our troubles. We know that he wants to bless us, and that he has, with many gifts and talents. I am certain most people would state that they trust God to hear them when they pray—but there seems to be a disconnect from our head to our feet. In our actions we try and solve all of our problems by innovative means, complaining when things don't go our way. We forego Mass and reconciliation because God will understand if we decide not to attend Mass. I remember hearing a priest at Mass speak to his congregation about this very subject. He said that many come to him for confession and say that they were unable to go to Mass while they were gone on vacation for the weekend. He responded with, "I bet you found the fine dining establishments. I bet you found the mall." His point was made and the congregation laughed in agreement. We really do find a way to be with family, go to the game, shop till we drop, but while our mouth says we find God to be important, our actions often bespeak the opposite. The more we believe the truth about God's love for us, that he cares for our past pains and is with us in our difficult present, the more we will demonstrate our belief with actions. This isn't about checking off Mass from our "to do" list; instead, it is about realizing our deep need to be fed by the "bread from heaven" and doing something that satisfies this need. It isn't about "having" to go to confession; rather, it is the realization that we often wander from God's love and he has done everything to provide a clear and clean path back to him.

It is this constant connection from our head to our feet, or the changing of our thinking so that we believe in a way that brings about holy actions, that allows us the platform to speak to others. We can't communicate about a relationship with Jesus if we don't have one with him. It is awfully difficult to insist others live a high standard of morality if we ourselves are struggling with immorality. The repulsion most of us have for hypocrisy keeps us from bragging about spiritual growth, but we must realize that those who are growing close to Jesus will have something to say to others, not because they have arrived, but because they see Jesus truly loving them and caring for them. What they have to say to others is not condemning, because they know how difficult it is to accept and live out a relationship with love. It is much easier to be a hypocrite, because it is the perfection of wearing a mask. For the person wanting an authentic relationship with God, hypocrisy is unappealing. When you see Jesus' love for you, you can share with others how great God's love truly is. This risking of ourselves to another's opinion by speaking about the way God has loved and helped us is part of the opportunity we have as Christians.

Vulnerability affects the relationships we have in our lives. It will test those relationships and can ultimately strengthen them. One day Linda shared with me that she struggled with a feeling of wanting to dress up and look good for her employer back when she was a full-time teacher. It really bothered her, but she risked her pride in order to open up about a personal struggle of wanting to gain his attention even though she was a married woman. That admission did two things. First, it depleted the power that the unconfessed struggle had in her life, and second, it opened an avenue of vulnerability and conversation between us that only strengthened our relationship. This open avenue of communication created an authentic platform for us to discuss something that was not easy to admit. I shared with her that I too had felt the same thing, in a number of ways. We truly were vulnerable with one another, and it has been a principle we have regularly developed over the years. I am confident that this openness has blocked many roads of greater selfishness.

You are not invited to speak about what you think holy folks want you to communicate. You are not called to pretend to be someone you are not. You are simply called to witness (martyr) to others what God has done in and for you. Risk it—I promise this is something you won't regret!

QUESTIONS

1. How do you present yourself to family and friends? Do you find that it is easy or hard to be yourself?

2. Do you feel God has given you specific gifts and talents? What are they?

3. Do you think you have invested those gifts in a way that is pleasing to God? Why?

4. What would happen if you shared with others how God has touched your life?

5. How has your vulnerability helped another to live his or her faith more authentically? How would that make you feel?

FURTHER READING

1. Parable of the talents: Matthew 25

2. Exodus 16

3. *Back to Virtue: Traditional Moral Wisdom for Modern Moral Confusion*, by Peter Kreeft

CHAPTER 9:
CHRIST IN US

My son seems to be athletically inclined, which I would love to take credit for, but I realize that my pear-shaped body has nothing to do with his athletic propensity. In fact, the other day a gathering of children began to do pull-ups, seeing who could do more, on a doorframe-mounted bar near the dining room. After my son did ten, one of the adults visiting our home asked how many I could do. I thought carefully and concluded that two was a probability. After all, I did have biceps hidden underneath the fat. So, with the plethora of children stepping aside, I jumped up and grabbed hold of the bar, defying gravity as I ascended to muscular greatness. I was confident I could muster together another pull-up, and just as I was about to go down for my next great lift, the whole bar disengaged from the doorframe and I fell, crashing onto the wooden floor. There was pain on my shin, and as I rolled on the ground, it seemed like I'd been kidney-punched by a heavyweight contender. As the entire table of adults sympathized with me with unadulterated laughter, I eventually gathered my body parts and pride together to go back to what I do best: sitting.

Last year I was able to attend one of my son's baseball games. I was running late but arrived just in time to see him making his way up to the plate for his turn at bat. I stood behind the cage, where I knew he could see me. My son was all business as he readied himself for the pitch. The swing connected perfectly with the ball, and he rocketed around the bases for a home run. I was so pumped! The other adults said I should stand behind him every time he hits, and I kept thinking, I made that kid. It was a wonderful moment.

This year my son jumped up a division and found himself one of the smallest kids on the team. His coach had played in the major league, so I told Noah that even if he didn't play a lot he certainly could learn a tremendous amount from this veteran player. The year passed by and he didn't have a lot of time on the field; in fact, he wasn't hitting the ball as effortlessly as he previously had. In the last game of the season, I arrived at the field near the end of the ninth inning, to find out that the team was losing pretty badly. My son hadn't played much at all during the game, but in the last inning the team seemed to rally and things were looking better. They were behind, but a couple of boys were on base, and with two outs, it was important to keep the momentum going. My son was called up to bat. I stood behind and watched, hoping for lightning to strike again. Strike one was soon followed by a second, as I anxiously awaited the next pitch. He could either keep the momentum going and potentially help win the game, or he would end their season. The last pitch was thrown, and my son struck out. The other team celebrated as Noah and his team got in line to congratulate them; they were going on to the playoffs.

As the teammates made their way to their parents, my son, with his head hung low, walked over to me. He was trying not to cry, but I could see that he was devastated. I put my arm around my boy and told him how proud I was of him, and that it wasn't his actions alone that had lost the game. He'd barely played during the season, and hadn't batted in the game thus far. He had been somewhat set up for failure, but in the end, he felt deeply what it means to lose. I walked with him toward home, encouraging and supporting him. He was my son, and I loved him whether he won or lost. He was someone I was proud of, regardless of the outcome of a particular game or moment at bat. I accepted him, and he needed that. We all need that.

The longing for acceptance, significance, and living life to the fullest is not an accidental desire within the human person. We are made with a hunger for answers and a propensity for asking big questions. This is God's gift to the human person, which inspires our longing for him. This union with our maker does not mean that the storms of life dissipate, nor that we will always feel emotionally strong. The gift of Christ so intimately given to us is a steadfast truth that does not depend upon an emotional response. The gift of his very self is so entire that he died to show us just how valuable we are to him. The love demonstrated, not simply spoken about, is without end in its application. We will always be his, because we were not carelessly created by God, nor were we haphazardly chosen by Christ. We have been truly seen by Jesus, and in that entire glance he invites us to stumble toward him, or even acknowledge our need for him in order to begin a new way of living.

What I love about Christianity is that Jesus takes us as we are, but then he enables us to be even more human in our willingness to follow him. Again, I can hear the cynical responses, maybe even some I've uttered myself, but Jesus' love for us is not conditional or hindered by cynicism. He loves us even if we don't love ourselves. He loves us when we have not demonstrated love toward others. Asking him to love us is almost an act of redundancy, because his whole earthly Incarnation is a declaration of his love for the human person. In our cry for healing and strength, from our broken promises and shattered lives, we are given a second chance. We truly can start over in Christ. I think this realization is key in how we interact with others. If we are wrapped up in despair or self-loathing, we have nothing to offer our fellow pilgrims. It is no wonder that many people claiming to know Christ have little impact in bringing others into the faith, because their words bespeak one thing and their actions another.

When I say that Jesus loves us entirely and gives everything so that we can truly start over, I am not saying this with a conditional clause hanging over everything. He loves you if . . . He forgives you everything but . . . He is calling you to follow him if you do this . . . Jesus sees us and calls us, but we have to want this new life; we have to see our need for a savior, or we won't seek him. "Ask and it will be given" is a promise we find in the Sacred Scriptures (see Luke 11:9). But we do have ask, because love does not force. Seek and you will find! Certainly, but that would mean we want to find answers. Knock and the door will be opened! Of course, but again, love will not manipulate you into this type of relationship. Jesus invites us to be forgiven, to be healed and whole, to an abundant life. What do you want?

A person who sees his or her past for what it really is, a time of often wandering into the thicket of life only to become pricked and poked, and battered and chased by the wolves of this world, will realize the joy of being found and rescued. This is the human condition—we are lost and need to be found. We are like those proverbial sheep who wander off and need the shepherd to come to our rescue. When this happens, something takes place in the heart of one who is found: gratitude. This is one reason why the Eucharist (which means "thanksgiving") is offered daily, because we daily must be willing to follow Jesus and be people who are thankful for such a new beginning.

To be grateful for all that Christ does will lead a person to a place of lived humility. We know that we can't fix ourselves, can't rescue or heal our friends, and can't start over in and of our own merit. Being the recipients of Jesus' generous offer of a new life does provide us the new start we so desperately long for, but it is easy to forget. When we forget we have been rescued, we become proud. When we forget that we were battered and hurt, we become insensitive to others who are broken. When we forget that Jesus chose us, we can become self-enclosed. And when we lose our gratitude, we lose our humility. When a person loses humility he sees others around him not as fellow travelers needing a helping hand, but as people who are inconvenient and who should certainly know better.

We can easily lose our gratitude if we are not careful to remind ourselves of the cross. Christ is now in us through baptism, and Jesus' unconditional love in our life frees us to love others who are unable to fix and heal themselves. What Jesus has done for us, he will certainly do for another, and this fact will show up in how we treat one another. Imagine if you were to be constantly belittled and reproved by Christ. This would do nothing to draw you to him; rather, you would likely flee to any other person in order to find acceptance. Why, then, knowing how much we need Jesus' unconditional love in our life, would we place stipulations upon others who need our love? Why would we withhold a generous act toward another, when Christ never held back his love for us? We will be effective and productive only when we center ourselves upon the cross of Christ, and stay there.

When we let Jesus meet our need, we will be able to accept and be present to others, who, like us, long to find peace. How many times have we striven to be accepted by others, pretended to be something we are not so that we could be included by family or friends? Too often we are unable to love people where they are, because we have not allowed Jesus to love us in the place that we find ourselves. I really believe the message for us to hold on to is that Jesus' unconditional love for us not only changes our future possibility, heals our past mistakes, and ministers to us in our present moment, but his provision enables us to be present with people, regardless of where they are on their spiritual journey. The reason so many people feel judged by others is probably because they really are being judged by others! It is difficult not to judge another who appears to have no interest in changing his or her life, which we see is obviously falling apart. It isn't easy to accept someone who repeatedly offends us without even realizing they are doing it.

While we cannot control others, insisting that they apologize for the hurts they have inflicted upon us or forcing them to be considerate and helpful, in the end we can make a choice in how we will interact with those we encounter today. It comes down to our own personal actions, and with Christ having done so much for us, even residing in us, we can bring healing to others and offer forgiveness.

What will you do today? When someone offends you, will you hold the grudge or realize that she is lost in her pain, hiding behind her walls? Will you say a kind word to someone who says something hurtful? We regularly tell our children to "kill them with kindness" when they have the unfortunate occasion to run into bullies, and maybe that is something we should try to practice. When a neighbor says the most inconsiderate thing on Facebook, do we go after him with both literary guns blazing, or do we turn the other cheek? We have a choice in how we deal with people who press all the wrong buttons. I have spent a lot of time trying to understand why someone says such hurtful things, when what I need to do is either ignore such juvenile behavior or find a way to show him or her through my response a better way. This is, of course, ideal behavior on our part. There will be good days and bad days, but I can say with certainty that knowing how much Christ has forgiven me, I need to apply that same attitude toward others. There will be times when we need to confront another who presses in and over our personal boundaries, but with a firm correction I need to also have an understanding heart. The boss who doesn't give the promised annual bonus may need to be spoken to, and it is likely that there are times when conditions at our places of employment become too difficult for us to continue working there, but the offending party is still a child of God who is lost.

Can you imagine how Jesus would respond to the person you have the most conflict with? Try and let Christ respond through you. How do we do that? I believe we simply ask Jesus to show us how much he loves us, and this can be the foundation for any communication we must have with the other person. Without the reminder of Jesus' love for us, we will resort to trying to handle the problem with our own strength, and usually that means responding to conflict with more conflict. As a father, there are times I can't believe how much my child overreacts to my instruction, but in my frustration I often find myself overreacting in return. Letting Jesus in me truly love family, friends, and strangers is the only way I will be able to press forward in these regular encounters with little regret. Love is not an emotional foundation, giving us warm feelings for those who are aggravating; rather, it is a tangible willed action, a choice to treat a person with dignity and respect even when he doesn't deserve it. We choose to extend to another what we would like for him to do to us—after all, it is fulfilling the Golden Rule. Part of the abundant life is moving and acting from gratitude, and doing so will be of more impact and effectiveness than trying to respond while relying on our own reservoirs of grace. That intolerable driver, waitress, or neighbor is often lost within his or her own personal hell, and our angry reactions will not change that person no matter how carefully crafted our internal monologue.

Love will change us, and it is the only thing that reaches the heart of those with whom we struggle. You have tried to solve it your way so many times before—why not let Christ in you respond to the difficult people and scenarios you find yourself in today? There is so much to be thankful for, and the joy of Christ in you is really all that you can center yourself upon. Christ in us enables us to truly love others.

I am pretty sure that Jesus laughed. I bet he laughed so hard that he doubled over and had trouble breathing. I think he told jokes, marveled at children as they got lost pretending, and maybe even smiles at us now. We need to relax and know that it truly is great to be human. Ask Jesus for that joy and perspective when you encounter difficult people. Who knows? Maybe you'll have something to smile about even if you lose the baseball game in the ninth inning.

QUESTIONS

1. If Christ is in you and he loves the whole world, how can you look at those you encounter differently?

2. If we cannot control others and the hurtful things they say, how can centering our lives on Christ's love for us impact those we encounter?

3. Is there someone you can offer forgiveness to today? Is it possible that someone you know is waiting for a healing word from you for a previous offense? What will you do?

4. How many times has Christ forgiven you? How can you let him offer forgiveness through you to those who offend you?

5. Think of the person you have the most difficulty with. Can you see him or her as having been made in God's image and likeness?

FURTHER READING

Galatians 2:20

CHAPTER 10:

THE CROSS

One of my favorite stories about the cross of Christ happened many years ago. I have a son named Kolbe (named after the saint and not the cheese). Kolbe has always approached life a bit differently than his other siblings. When he turned five he declared, "I'm done with my fours now." While eating dinner at an Outback Steakhouse, little three-year-old Kolbe, holding his french fry dripping with ketchup, carried on his lunch with this dialogue: "Noooooo, don't eat me." He has always made us laugh, and it seems he was born with an active imagination. One day I was doing a number of talks in a church in Pennsylvania and brought my family along to keep me company. The day ended with Mass. As I gathered my family near the front of the church, little Kolbe sat next to me and seemed fixated on the gigantic crucifix hanging from the wooden beams above the altar. The corpus on the cross was rather large, and in many ways extremely beautiful. Kolbe looked up at me and simply said: "Jesus." It was very cute, and I nodded back to him, affirming that it was Jesus hanging upon the cross. In a lot of ways I began to feel really great about myself—after all, my son knew who

Jesus was. He was so bright, so holy, and surely this was a sign that he was going to be an amazing priest one day. I was lost in thoughts of the great Kolbe Padgett's sanctity, concluding that it really did make sense that he would understand so much at such a young age. After all, we had crucifixes in our home, tons of rosaries, and statues aplenty as constant opportunities for visual catechesis. I travel all over the world sharing the story of Jesus' love, so why wouldn't he be so aware of the beauty of the cross? I said, "Yes, Kolbe, that's Jesus." He looked up at me and asked, "What's he doing here?" I was momentarily at a loss for words. I looked at my son, realizing I wasn't as amazing a parent as I'd just imagined, and responded with, "He lives here. He's in the tabernacle. He's in our hearts." Kolbe responded, "How'd he get in here?" By that time, the lady who'd invited me in to speak, who was sitting behind me, was doubled over with laughter, almost rolling on the floor.

The cross is something we may have seen our whole lives, but do we understand why it is so important? Have we found ourselves clinging to the cross of Christ, knowing that his death is our beginning, that his sacrifice is our healing? We must talk about the cross in order to understand the abundant life we are invited to experience.

The cross is a central sign and symbol revered within Christianity. Catholics and Protestants alike value and speak about the cross and what happened there so long ago. The Catholic cross has the corpus of Christ still upon it, and at times some of these artistic renditions of the "great exchange" can be very bloody. Why are we so fixated upon such a morbid act? Why would we willingly place bejeweled crosses around our necks, as if this horrible means of death is something to cherish? It is an ironic accessory if one really thinks about the type of death experienced upon those two wooden beams. The cross has always been important for Christians because, while it is a place of bloodshed and extreme suffering, it is the manner in which Jesus Christ chose to demonstrate just how much he was willing to endure so that we could be saved. Outside the Biblical context, the cross could easily be placed amid many other means of torture and death, but seen in the light of salvation history, Jesus' complete gift of self upon the cross transforms our lives once and for all.

In the Old Testament there is a classic story of Isaac being taken by his father, Abraham, to Mount Moriah to be offered as sacrifice to the Lord (Genesis 22). Most people remember this story because it is where Abraham begins to tie his son up in order to offer him as a sacrifice to God. We realize later, from the letter to the Hebrews, that Abraham believed even if Isaac was slain the Lord would raise him up. Even in the Old Testament account Abraham tells the servants with him that he and the boy will go up and return. The faith Abraham has in God is certainly tested to the maximum limit, but he remains steadfast in his belief that God will keep his promises in spite of appearances. As most of us know, the Lord provided a ram who was caught in the thicket, and Isaac was spared. What I find to be of great significance is Isaac's willingness to allow his father to bind his hands and feet without the slightest opposition. We see the son trusting his father so completely that there isn't even a single protest. Certainly Isaac could run from the mountain away from potential harm, and he could easily overpower his father, who is an old man at this time, but he doesn't. Isaac willingly offers himself into his father's hands.

Correlate this to Jesus at the cross, who willingly allows his hands and feet to be bound to the wood with nails. Think of Jesus, who implicitly trusts his father and says, "Into your hands I commit my spirit." Jesus is the fulfillment of that Old Testament type, and that offered sacrifice solidified the covenant God had made throughout all of salvation history. In the Old Testament the blood of lambs and bulls would be shed to offer on behalf of the sinful Israelites, but it wouldn't forgive their sins. Jesus is the lamb of God whose blood is shed on behalf of sinful humanity but is also capable of forgiving sin.

Remember the story of Moses delivering the children of Israel from Egyptian captivity? The final plague that allowed Israel to leave Egypt was the slaughter of the firstborn son (Exodus 12). The only way to avoid this horrific death was to take a spotless lamb, place the blood from its sacrifice over the doorposts, and then consume the lamb as a meal. Jesus, as the Lamb of God, sheds his blood, and it is placed over the door of our hearts. We must also eat the lamb, which we certainly do at every Mass. The cross is the place where all the Old Testament prophesies, covenants, and types come to fulfillment. The cross, with its painful and bloody death, is the place where the son of promise willingly places himself into the Father's hands so that sacrifice can be offered, once for all, for you and me. The cross is where the old way of living ends, the captivity and enslavement of sin is broken, the tyrannical rule of Satan is shattered, and the sting of death is removed. The cross is what we place before our eyes, so that we don't forget that we needed a Savior.

What I love about the crucifix is that there is a body intentionally visible upon the wooden beams. As Catholics, we revere and celebrate the Resurrection with vigor; it's called Easter! The corpus is on the cross to remind us that Jesus really was a man who bled, who did feel the pain of the thorns violently placed upon his head. Jesus really did feel the scourge as it mangled and bloodied his back, and he felt the weight of the cross as he carried it to Calvary. The crucifix has the corpus on it so that we don't make it only another accessory to our outfits, so that we don't simply conclude that it is a traditional decoration, and so that we don't forget our sin is worthy of real death. The cross is the place where love is demonstrated most vividly, because Jesus didn't have to agree to that type of death. Jesus wasn't a victim, nor was he under the delusion that he had no other option but to submit to the corrupt world power. He willingly took all of that pain and suffering to show us—not just tell us—that a relationship with the human person is worth every lash of the whip, every jeer of the crowd, every stroke of the hammer upon the nail. We were of worth to God, and so he offered everything for us!

Often when we hear the readings in church about the person who finds the pearl of great price, or sells all he has in order to gain it, we think that this is a story told for us to hold dearly the truth of Jesus' love. While this is true, I think it also speaks about God's heart for us. He is the one who searched for us, as if we were a lost coin. We are the ones he went after, the lamb who wandered away from the others. We are the pearl of great price that God sought out and gave all in order to purchase. Why would he consider us of such worth, we who willingly spat upon his claims of kingship, who thrust the spear into his side in order to commit deicide? Why would he care for such an ungrateful creation? Jesus articulates it to us from the cross: "Father forgive them for they know not what they do." (Luke 23:34) Jesus knows that sin has clouded our vision, that pride has distanced our hearts from him, and he knows that we don't understand what love looks like. He understands that we are inclined to a life of selfishness and disordered passions, and so he comes to show us what an abundant life can look like. Jesus shows us that to really live is to serve others, to sacrifice for the betterment of our fellow human beings, to intercede for them even if they are unappreciative. He shows us that fighting so that others can become whole is a fight worthy of one's entire gift of self. The cross is where selflessness overcomes selfishness. The cross is where sacrifice and service make null and void self-gratification and pride. The cross is where we see what the love of God looks like in time!

The cross is so important that Saint Paul said he determined to know nothing among them except Jesus Christ and him crucified (1 Corinthians 2:2). Paul told the Galatians that he was crucified with Christ and the life he now lived he lived by faith in the Son of God (Galatians 2:20). In other words, the cross changed everything about how Paul lived his life and how he interacted with others. Saint Peter would tell the recipients of his letter that the reason people are ineffective and unproductive in the faith is because they have forgotten that they were cleansed from their past sins (2 Peter 1). Keeping the cross at the forefront of our minds and in the manner in which we live will help us to be the most authentic persons we could ever hope to be. Why? Because holding the cross close to our hearts and willingly dying to our disordered passions and selfish tendencies not only ensures that we are following Jesus and not the world, the flesh, and the devil, but it also ensures that we will truly live the life we were created to live. The cross is where we die to our self-love and receive real love. The receptivity of the love of Christ and the loss of our introspective obsessing doesn't take away from our true expression; rather, it enables us to truly be ourselves. Jesus invites us to follow him, and so we are told to daily take up our cross. Why daily? Because, like the manna provided for the Israelites in the wilderness, God wants us to depend on him every day. We can certainly choose to do it our own way, pursuing selfish ends and giving in to any of the desires that make an appearance, but we will not be truly free. Sin enslaves, while love liberates. Sin takes us back to the captivity of our distorted human expression, while the cross frees us up to enter the Promised Land whole and at peace.

In our home we have crucifixes everywhere. The constant reminder of God's love for us is on display in most every room, but we will not be different if we only see it as decoration. We will be different if we realize that Jesus' complete gift of self is a declaration for all time that God has sought us out, even when we wouldn't seek him. God has considered us of invaluable worth, even when we didn't see him to be worth our time and talents. God makes us an offer today—will we accept the invitation to be in a relationship of love with him?

When we talk about the cross, can you think of selfish areas in your life that need to be offered to Jesus? Dying to our selfishness isn't a feeling we try and muster up; rather, it is an intentional willing of virtue over the particular vice. Let's say you have a desire for a clean house, but the children have decided to do everything in their power to counter your efforts. While it is normal to want to scream at the little mess-makers, by instead placing our frustration upon the cross we are willing a holy response over an unholy one. When our fantasy football team is anything but the fantasy we would like them to be, reminding ourselves that eternity isn't in the hands of our quarterback could be a small act of dying. When your employees don't send out the proper order and you find yourself on the other end of an angry client's phone call, all of that frustration can be united to the cross and become a gift to Jesus for another's betterment. It's true that to approach difficulties and hurts with this perspective is not our first response, but it is the one that will over time change us into the holy men and women God is calling us to be. In every moment of your day you can unite your struggles to the cross, place your disordered desires on the cross you must carry, and learn a new way of living that not only makes you a better person but also changes the lives of those you care about.

I really want to challenge you to try this approach in the coming days. If you are willing to have the cross centered in your mind throughout your day, the problems and struggles will be placed into the context that brings life. The idea of dying to disordered desires is not made once and for all on our part; rather, it is a daily choice to let the work of Christ become active in each of our moments. Haven't we all tried to deal with frustrations in a reactionary way enough to know that it does not help us be the best we can be? What will happen if we try a new approach, the way of the cross?

Most of you are tired, but not because you have failed God so miserably that you are beyond healing and hope. It isn't God who has given up on you; rather, it is you who have given up on yourselves. Jesus is not intolerant of you for trying and failing, for screaming when you should have been calm, or for struggling with lust when you really wanted to be pure. Jesus has not given up on you because you were tempted and gave in to a vice. The love Christ has for us is certainly not granting permission to gratify the self and give in to disordered desire, or encouraging us to remain in our vice, but often our fall is grounded in a false understanding of God's love. This false understanding is what the cross remedies. Jesus loves us even if we fall, and he loves us even when we misunderstand, but he will always invite us to look once again at what he has done, so that we can see what we can do.

What can we do? We can be saints. We can have victory where we have struggled before. We can live a new life, instead of remaining trapped. Jesus is not waiting for us to fall so he can give up on us. The motivation for living a new life is seeing the cross for what it really is, an entire demonstration of self-sacrifice for us so that we can know that we are loved. The more we realize this truth, the more we will live in a way that we most desire. As we reflect upon the cross, Jesus' love for us becomes keenly emphasized in our thinking and it will result in a desire for good over the vices we previously entertained.

You are loved by God. This love from God to you is not predicated upon your ability to live a specific amount of virtue; instead, it is grounded in who he is. Learning more about how much God loves you will change your outlook on life. This personal outlook will not grow in virtue if you are lost in regret, paralyzed with fear, and worried you cannot perform up to his heavenly standards. It is true that Jesus doesn't want us to yell at our kids, steal from the company, ignore those in need, and give in to despair, but he is not giving up on you when you fall into these moments of sin. The cross shows us that God is not willing that any should perish, but that all be given the chance to truly live. Let the cross of Christ remind you that you can start over today. If you think about this gift of absolute love from Jesus more often, I know you will not only see a change in your personal life, but you will find living without regret far more enjoyable than you ever imagined. The more you fix your eyes upon the cross of Christ, the more you will realize that the answer to the question "What's he doing here?" is that he is trying to show you just how much he thinks of you.

QUESTIONS

1. How can the Old Testament stories about Abraham and Isaac, and Moses and Israel be examples of the types of love Jesus has demonstrated for us?

2. What selfish acts can you place upon the cross you carry daily?

3. How can you change your vices into virtues?

4. Why do we emphasize the crucifix so much in our spiritual development?

5. Will you let Jesus love you today? How can this help you face difficult moments?

FURTHER READING

1. *A Father Who Keeps His Promises: God's Covenant Love in Scripture*, by Scott Hahn

CONCLUSION

So, you actually read this book? I am glad you picked it up and am hopeful you found out that even with all your flaws, God is captivated by you. Even though you aren't OK, it still really is OK, because God had a plan all along. When the enemy tried to sidetrack you with your difficult past, God had a plan!

As I wrap things up, I'd like to leave you with a few concluding remarks, because obviously the previous chapters didn't get it all out of my system! I figured it wouldn't hurt to say it one last time: You are loved, just the way you are. I know that sounds like a cliché, but this proclamation of unconditional love is what I believe is necessary for each individual to become the best expression our humanity will allow, and it is what we've often forgotten in our religious pursuits. Don't get sidetracked by the world with its glam and glitz. Try and stay centered on Jesus when people who should know better do things that hurt. You can't change everyone so that they'll do the right thing instead of the wrong, but at least you have the opportunity to let Jesus make you more sensitive to his love. I guess I just don't want you to give up. I feel a little like a parent watching his small child go off to school for the first time. I am aware of the bullies you'll encounter over the years, the difficulty of the classroom dynamics, and the weight of the course load. I know many who have gotten overwhelmed by it all, and I don't want you to think you are alone.

Jesus is not trying to trick you, or waiting for you to trip and fall so he can move on to someone holier. Our Lord is captivated with you! So, when you find yourself alone and tired, invite Jesus into that moment. I know it will be hard, and probably even more difficult the closer you run to Jesus. Why? Because walking in opposition to the world and its demands isn't easy, nor is the flesh ready to just fall into step with your newfound emphasis on faith. The enemy of our soul is going to pick up his diabolical efforts to make you believe that trying to live for Christ is hopeless. With the difficulties you face, the Spirit of God is there to comfort you. Jesus will not abandon you, and hasn't left you orphaned. You are beloved by God and even if all hell comes after you, the victory you gain in Christ is greater than the world, the flesh, and the devil. I am cheering you on!

So I will leave you with an opportunity: Will you continue to beat yourself up for the struggles you experience in this life, or will you stand in opposition to the temptation to despair and embrace your redeemed humanity? Will you allow others to see that you are not OK, but that it is truly OK because of Jesus' love for you? If you are open to standing against this tendency to pretend all is fine or to give in to despair because of your faults, then I believe people will be interested in knowing the Jesus you know. Why? Because people want to be loved and accepted just as they are. Christ has accepted us just as we are, and it is now OK. This is a message worth sharing.

What do we do now? We need to think and act differently than we have up until this point. We can't continue to do the same thing we have done year after year and assume that we will see different results—that is the definition of insanity. We need to approach this matter of our need for Christ, and allow Jesus to daily come and meet us where we are. We must cling to the cross and gain the heavenly perspective, because through our Lord's gift we are being prepared to spend forever with him. Allowing Jesus to come into the area of our life that is not OK will impact the role of community and fellowship in the body of Christ, the Church. This is a holy opportunity we have been given, because our choices will motivate others. Christianity is grounded in the person of Jesus Christ, and he has never been afraid of our wounds and deep want for meaning. Jesus is never upset that we are not OK, and he is never tired of offering us healing and forgiveness. He looks at the mother who is exhausted from all her responsibilities and frustrations, and affirms her sacrificial act. He sees the efforts of frazzled students and offers them strength. Our Lord knows the disappointments found in our unmet goals and unfulfilled dreams. Jesus invites us to receive acceptance from him and then to offer to others what we have found: real love.

The other day I called my parish to see if confession was still being offered at the normal time on Saturday afternoon. I called because it was the Christmas season and sometimes our regular routines have different schedules at the church. The priest answered the call and said there wasn't confession that Saturday. I hung up the phone feeling a little bummed because I'd hoped to offer Jesus a bit cleaner version of my messy self.

Fifteen minutes later my cell phone rang and my parish priest said, "Chris, if you want to come to confession, meet me in the rectory at eleven thirty a.m." I was dumbfounded. First, I hadn't told him who I was. Second, my cell number has a Florida area code, so it wasn't as if he could have easily deduced it was me. Third, I didn't think my voice was that recognizable. Good grief! As I entered the rectory, I felt such gratitude and mercy that my priest would make the effort to find me and call me in order to offer me healing through the sacrament of reconciliation. I had an amazing confession and Jesus healed my broken heart. Jesus knows our voice; he knows our need and he is ready to seek us out so that we can be whole. I think my priest was a perfect example of the love Christ has for all of us. Jesus knows we are not OK, and that is why he comes to us, to help us heal and know what it is like to truly be loved, just as we are. Just so you know, I'm still not OK, and neither are you. But it's OK!

QUESTIONS

1. What are you going to do now?

FURTHER READING

1. Start over and read this book again. I think it will offer you a few new reminders.

THE
DYNAMIC CATHOLIC
INSTITUTE

[MISSION]

To re-energize the Catholic Church in America by developing world-class resources that inspire people to rediscover the genius of Catholicism.

[VISION]

To be the innovative leader in the New Evangelization helping Catholics and their parishes become the-best-version-of-themselves.

DynamicCatholic.com
Be Bold. Be Catholic.®

The Dynamic Catholic Institute
5081 Olympic Blvd
Erlanger, Kentucky 41018
Phone: 859-980-7900
Email: info@DynamicCatholic.com